Praise for *The*

"Julie has knocked it out of the park in *The Right Time Is Right Now*. only provides the inspiration for creating a better life, but also actual action steps to help readers start making changes now, not 'someday.' I highly recommend this book; it's a must-read!"

–Todd Patkin, Happiness Expert, author of *Finding Happiness*

"If you've dreamed of going off on a weekend retreat to clear your head, charge your batteries, and move forward with confidence, Julie McGrath's book is the next best thing (and a lot more frugal!). Using her expertise, she challenges and coaches with care as she helps you carve a path to a happier, healthier life."

–Jill Geisler, Loyola University Chicago, author of
Work Happy: What Great Bosses Know

"The *Right Time Is Right Now* is not your usual self-help book…not by a long shot! Julie offers six questions that ask the reader to ponder and respond truthfully. By sharing stories from those who have overcome fears, lack self-confidence, or face physical challenges, she guides the reader through gentle steps and tips. This is sure to be a 'go-to' book when you're feeling down, overwhelmed or in need of a nudge to get yourself motivated."

–Sallie Felton, Professional Life Coach

Published by
The Joy Source, LLC
2 Bourbon Street
Peabody, MA 01960

First edition: March 2017
Editor: Kate Victory Hannisian, Blue Pencil Consulting
Book and Cover Design: Lisa McKenna, Curious Marie, LLC
Printing: King Printing Co., Inc.
Author Photos: ©Ayles Photography (PAGE 112) and ©Island Photography (BACK COVER)

ISBN: 978-0-9884788-2-4

To:
Bridget
This is the
right time for
you! Love Diana 3/17

To Elisa, my true friend and confidante

Table of Contents

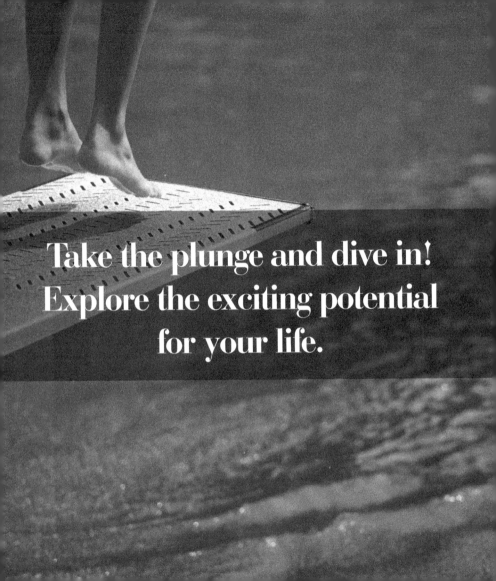

Take the plunge and dive in! Explore the exciting potential for your life.

Introduction

Welcome to *The Right Time Is Right Now*! This book is a call to action. If you are busy but know you need some help steering your life in a better, more fulfilling direction, you're in luck, because I made this book short and sweet on purpose. Each short chapter gets right to the point, giving you hints, tips, guidance and inspiration. Read this book, once or a hundred times, to help you unlock your potential to create the life you have always wanted and dreamed about! My goal is to guide you, nudge you and help you realize what is missing from your life or getting in the way of creating the life you have always wanted. This book will prompt you to review your friendships, how you spend your time, and your goals by asking you simple yet direct questions. I won't change your life, but *you* can change your life! No more excuses, start today! If you answer "no" to any of the six key questions, even just one of them, this book is for you!

The shift in your life will happen when you can answer all six of these questions with a big, exciting YES! You will notice positive changes even as you get to one YES. In fact, **even as you work towards YES, your life will shift in the direction you want it to go.**

I wrote this book because I have worked with hundreds of women (and men, too!) who are struggling with the questions I ask you in this book. I've heard all the excuses and the major challenges that prevent people from accomplishing their goals and living up to their true potential. One major theme I hear from so many people is that it never seems to be the "right" time to begin working on themselves and their lives. I've heard every excuse you can imagine, from being "too busy" to "not enough money" or "waiting for life to get easier." Know this: The longer you wait, the harder it will be. I realize that so people many don't know what is wrong in their lives — how can you change what you don't know? You can't, so month after month, year after year, not much has changed for the better. You may find you just keep doing the same old thing and expect different results, only to be frustrated, let down, and simply annoyed when nothing seems to go your way.

That's why for this book, I break down the change process into a series of questions. As you go through the book and answer these questions, you may find that some questions raise issues you might be coping with just fine, while others might spotlight issues that require extra attention, reflection, and hard work to gain deep insight. I'll ask you many questions throughout each chapter to help you get clear about what you want in life. As you ask yourself these questions, let the process stir up some answers for you! These may be easy questions to ask yourself, but it may be difficult to figure out why you are not doing what you could be doing to create a better life.

I invite you to take the plunge and dive in! Explore your endless possibilities and the exciting potential for your life. Start asking yourself these questions and grab your journal to write down your answers. Or use this book to record your answers. (There's no "right" or "wrong" way to use this book, but if you use a journal to record your answers you can revisit this guide over and over again as you need to.)

You'll notice that I've asked each of the six questions in the first person. That's because I want you to "hear" yourself ask these very important questions in your own voice. A favorite quote forever embedded in my heart is "If I do not go within, I go without." This book will require you to go within, and to engage in some inner dialogue and reflection. I'm asking you these questions, but I don't know what your answers will be. I only know that by answering them you will get to a better place or, at the very least, understand where the problems or "stuck" points lie in your life.

If you don't go within, how will you know what you are going without? How do you know you are truly happy with the work you do, with the friendships you keep? The book's questions might also challenge you on topics like where and how you spend your time. Your challenge may be to seek alternate routes in your life, rekindle long-lost friendships, or take your old dreams off the shelf and put them back into action.

How will you know what is right for you? Take some time, preferably uninterrupted time (even short, 15-minutes sessions) to dive in. After all, time doesn't wait for you, which is why I named the book *The Right Time Is Right Now*. I encourage you to take the time to reflect on these questions and go inward for the answers. What are your expectations for your life? What are your priorities? Learning and growing? Challenging yourself? Brilliant! The first step is understanding where you are in your life today. How are your confidence and self-esteem?

Do you believe you deserve a great life? If you do, this book is for you. Many people accept stress, chaos and boredom as a way of life. I challenge you to refuse to accept that way of thinking. Instead, think of calm, fulfillment and happiness as a way of life you not only deserve but are willing to make an effort to achieve. Put that effort in today. The right time is right now. Why wait?

Don't wait to change your lifestyle until the doctor tells you to get healthier — and you are 75 and feeling awful. Don't wait to be financially secure before you allow yourself to be happy, and in the meantime carry the burden of debt and all the harmful byproducts of stress it can cause you. Please know that waiting and putting off what is so vital to your happiness can turn into a big, huge mistake — and damage your current life satisfaction and happiness. Start now, and let this book lead the way!

Julie McGrath

Am I Engaged in Work that I Love?

1

Ask yourself these questions. Write your answers down in your journal or in this book, or just think them through, whatever works for you.

- Am I engaged in work that I love?

  ....

  ....

  ....

- What do you do?

  ....

- Are you doing what you do, not out of love,
  but because it's all you know?

  ....

- Are you doing what you love part-time? What's the missing piece that would get you there all of the time (if that's what you want)?

  ....

  ....

  ....

- What are the obstacles?

  ....

  ....

  ....

- Are you stopping at *good enough*?

  ....

- Are you blessed to be doing exactly what you want to be doing every day for work and/or pleasure?

....

....

- Do you wake up every day (okay, most days) thrilled to go to work or use your talents in some way that makes you a better person?

....

....

- Do you get to put your talents to work, making you feel successful and empowered?

....

Or are you watching someone else, your spouse or a friend perhaps, do what they love? Somehow, day after day of helping them reach *their* full potential has put you on the sidelines of your own life, leaving you feeling a bit sour and restless. You ask: When is my time?

Suppose I said to you, *now is the right time.* What would you say? "No way, I need to wait for a better time?" When is a better time? Will that time come? Will you know when it comes? If you have sacrificed your own dreams for the good of someone else, and you are watching their smiles and increased joy in life, now it's your time to get some joy of your own.

• •

Here's the bottom line: When you are doing something that you love, you feel good. You are happier and more invested in your life.

• •

If you are in a place of hating your everyday routine, you cannot help but feel drained and frustrated. If you are living for the weekends and dreading the weekdays (or the opposite), let this thought resonate within you. It doesn't have to be that way. What if you felt great about what you do *every day*? If that thought overwhelms you because it would mean making some big or small changes in your life, hold that thought and keep on reading. This book walks you through creating the life you love!

Remember, I have heard every excuse about why you can't get started, every single excuse. Some are genuine, hard roadblocks, and others are obstacles created by your thoughts and actions. Please know I understand how situations arise where you can't remember how you got there. I understand how one day you wake up and look in the mirror and say, "I can't stand this anymore, something has to change." If this sounds like where you are right now, you have found the right book! I will offer you the steps you need to guide you to a place of loving what you do! There's plenty of joy to go around, so grab some for yourself. It might mean you have to put new plans and goals into your life. What you are meant to do, "your God-given talent," is waiting for you! Discover it, do it, align yourself with it, and your life will change in amazing ways.

If you don't know what I mean and you need a visual, go find someone who is doing what they love! If you are thinking, "Well, I used to love what I chose to do and now I don't," that's okay. Please don't pretend not to know how you are feeling; instead, acknowledge it and sit with it. Make a decision to make a change, or at least work towards one! Often times many of us make what we believe is the right choice that will bring us satisfaction and joy. And it does most of the time, but at a certain point the "right choice" can change because *we change*!

· ·

We might want more, need more and become more aligned
with ourselves and what brings us happiness
and what no longer serves us.

· ·

Let's Get Honest About Work

Since we spend the majority of our waking hours working, it is vital to be doing so engaged in work that nourishes us. Ask yourself these questions about your work:

- Is it a job you enjoy? ☐ yes ☐ no ☐ sometimes

- Are you working in a job you are good at? ☐ yes ☐ no

- If you don't enjoy it, when did you stop enjoying it or lose interest?

- Did something happen to make you dissatisfied?

- What's lacking? Workplace camaraderie? Pay? Excitement? A tolerable commute? Something else?

  ....

  ....

  ....

- What are you doing about it?

  ....

  ....

  ....

- Are you looking for and finding a new job?   ☐ yes   ☐ no

  ....

- Going back to school to complete a degree or acquire new skills? ☐ yes ☐ no

  ....

- Complaining and doing nothing? (This is the easiest choice, but it's generally not the right one.)

  ....

- What would you *like* to do?

  ....

  ....

- What is causing you not to change your circumstance? Fear? Lack of motivation? Is moving out of your comfort zone hard? Yes, it is — but it's worth it!

  ....

  ....

  ....

- If you are staying home instead of going to a workplace (stay-at-home parent, retired) are you doing so by choice? Your choice? Is this what you love?

....

....

....

If you are home all day, whether by choice or not, you need to make good use of your time. What are you doing that you *love*? If you are a stay-at-home parent, what are you doing when you kids are not home that calls to your strengths? This can be a trap for people who believe that their kids will fill them up with everything they would ever need. It is also very draining (as I explored in my first book, *Joy-Worthy*) and I see it all the time. While the kids are in school, the mother shops, cleans, and hangs out on Facebook, and then when the kids return home she has little positive momentum to keep her going and immediately feels drained.

Find something that stimulates you and gives you purpose. Stop pretending you are happy if you are not. Some of us try really hard to convince others that we are happy when we are the farthest thing from it. What a burden that must be, to suffer in silence! After all, if you don't feel worthy of a great life, you won't get one! You need to *want* to be nourished and fulfilled, and *want that for yourself!* Believe you are worthy of feeling amazing and doing what you love. Some of us are internally driven by issues or circumstances beyond our control, perhaps things that happened to us as children. What you don't deal with as you get older is still within you and manifests in different ways. You have to get to a place where you feel good enough, whole, complete, and solid. If you are not at that place, you must put in the requisite amount of time to change your feelings. You cannot "outgrow" your issues by simply burying them.

Self-Esteem and Its Impact on Your Choices

Self-esteem and self-confidence are emotional drivers behind every choice you make and just about every single thing you do in your life. As you read this book and ask yourself the questions, you'll accomplish very little if you don't look at your self-esteem first and foremost. I would be steering you in the wrong direction if I told you otherwise. Low self-esteem translates into negative self-talk, and you will talk yourself right out of a great life. Those negative thoughts will tell you what you are capable of and what you shouldn't do, and they will drive what you will accomplish. Think of all the good stuff you are missing out on! If you want your dreams and goals to come to fruition, you must get to a place of saying to yourself, "I can do it," or "I'm going to do it," or "if it doesn't work out, I know I tried my best." If you are not at this place of confidence, keep reading, I have some ideas for you.

Building self-esteem is a lifelong process. Some of us were not lucky enough to be born into families with high self-esteem, in fact, some of us were born into families with dysfunction and fear. These issues can stand in the way of you seeking a good life.

Think about your sense of self. How do you feel about yourself?

- Do you like yourself?
  ....
  ....

- Can you sit alone and enjoy your own company?
  ....

- Did something happen when you were younger (or later on in your life) to damage your sense of self-worth? Did you bury it?
  ....
  ....
  ....

- Do you get triggered by people or places that instantly lower your self-esteem?
  ....
  ....

When your self-esteem is low, you can become complacent and stuck in your comfort zone. Your issues can find you at whatever point in life, and sometimes we get triggered by a past hurt or just live with a damaged sense of self, which permeates everything we attempt to do. Low self-esteem can also manifest in how you raise your children. Do you live through them? Do you want them to excel at everything, and often find yourself bragging about all they do for a hint of validation that yes, they are "good enough," which really stems from your feelings of being "not good enough" yourself?

Get to a point in your life where no outside validation is necessary. You know you are good enough.

How you deal with constructive criticism or adversity directly relates to how you feel about yourself. If you already don't feel good enough, you will react strongly and take every critical word personally. If you (or your kids) are not included in an event, you will feel hurt and angry, going back to your low self-esteem. This is wasted time and energy spent on the wrong feelings. Jealously, anger, and revenge are all feelings that won't uplift you! Those negative feelings certainly won't help you create the life you want. Like attracts like; I am a strong believer in what you think so hard about is what gets created in your life.

Work to get your self-esteem up. Surround yourself with positive, solid, stable people you want to emulate. Watch how they navigate life. It will rub off on you if you let it. In fact, I've devoted a whole chapter of the book to this very subject of surrounding yourself with positive people.

How to work on your self-esteem? Move out of denial, because ignorance is not bliss. If you have deep issues, find a therapist to speak to and work on them. It can be a slow, painful process depending on your issues, but worth every minute. You will emerge into the light stronger and more resilient. Take the time to work on it. If you are always moving and never slowing down, is that a sign that you fear if you stop and think you will realize you may not be happy with your current situation, people, life, and work?

Stop. Breathe. You have everything you need inside yourself to make changes. Speak to someone who is trained professionally to help you deal with whatever you may need to talk about. For my stubborn readers, yes, just give it a try! Trained professionals can help you. It may be that you need to find the right fit or connection with someone in the mental health field, but there are plenty of professionals to choose from. What you discuss with therapists is confidential and they are nonjudgmental. Even if you simply need a little "tune-up" on how you are doing in your life, it's worth it!

Self-Esteem Boosters

Here's a starter list of ways to boost your self-esteem:

- Therapy!
- Discover what you are good at doing and go do it!
- Focus on the positive, not on the negative.
- Exercise.
- Eat healthy.
- Cut out of your life what doesn't make you feel good (cigarettes, alcohol, drugs, mean people).

When you live your life from a place of solid self-esteem and self-worth, everything becomes possible. You see the world differently and the world experiences you as empowered and strong. Stop blaming. Stop being the victim. Be realistic and honest about how you feel.

....
It's okay to not be okay with your current situation.
....

In fact, the only way you will make any changes is when you admit that to yourself. Many of us change direction all through our lives to get to a better spot. It's good that you try, but you need to know when it's not working for you. The more you sit with fake feelings, the more you are losing out; and losing out is not getting you to a place of joy and contentment. Instead, it's sitting with smoldering sadness and denial.

When you don't love what you do, you can become depressed and stressed. Then stress opens the door for many unhealthy habits. Think about it. How do you cope when every day is a bore? Many people choose the unhealthy ways to deal; drugs, alcohol, sleeping pills, fatty foods, cigarettes… and the list goes on and on. Unfortunately, you can lose the desire to want more in your own life. Once you are beaten down by life, depression follows. Loss of hope and motivation becomes closer to you than hope and excitement. It's like giving up on "what could be" and settling for "what is," even when "what is" is not even satisfactory.

Choose hope! Make the choice to move forward in search of what you love! Choose the healthy way to deal! Now is the right time to change course, and get excited to actually think about doing what you love every day!

Life coach and speaker Kim Ravida frequently works with people on how to make the correct moves in their life based on their goals and dreams, Here's what she says about fear, a major topic for people who just can't seem to move out of their comfort zone to grasp what they need:

"The interesting thing is most people won't say they are afraid of something specific; instead, fear shows up in very interesting ways. Fear can show up in ways such as piling too much on yourself to do. If you have big to-do lists and a jam-packed schedule, you'll never get to anything and that actually keeps you safe. However, when you have too much to do, it's almost impossible to finish any one thing.

Ask yourself: are you keeping yourself (because make no mistake, it is you that is doing this) so busy because you absolutely have to do these things, or are they holding you back from achieving what it is you want? Be completely honest with your answer here, because often we think we have to do things or should do things when we really don't."

Cell Phone Pitfalls

A note about the cell phones and smartphones that so many of us keep constantly in our hands or by our sides. These marvelous devices have many beneficial uses, but an unfortunate side effect is that they have taken away our potential reflection time and replaced it with constant chatter. If you are serious about making thoughtful changes in your life, change your relationship with your phone. When you don't have to bring it with you, look at it, or be on it, don't. Pass up the chance to bring it with while you are waiting for an appointment and start up a conversation with someone instead. Sit in quiet and think about your life, and whether you are doing what you love. Look around, is this where you want to be? The phone won't be a great place to get those answers. The device is always connected and can tell you the latest score of the hockey game, which Hollywood star is dating who, or the weather, but it can't tell you how you feel and what you need to do to get moving to improve your life. These deep answers come from an uncluttered mind. Don't let the phone or the computer be the default on your boring or unchallenged life. That is too easy! And the rewards are zero! Wait, let me say this one more time, just to be sure you heard me correctly:

•••••••••••••••••••••••••••••••••••••••

Don't let the phone or the computer be the default on your boring or unchallenged life. That is too easy! And the rewards are zero!

•••••••••••••••••••••••••••••••••••••••

Sitting back and watching life pass you by is easy. Watching your friend go back to school is easy. Keeping busy so you don't have time to actually think about whether you are doing what you love is easy. Living vicariously through your children is easy. Let's face it, easy is tempting and can lure us away from even our best intentions. We need to pass up easy for challenging, because nothing gets done when you choose the easy way out.

Do you find yourself saying any of the following phrases, and how do you complete them?

- I always wanted to do
  ....

- I was always interested in
  ....

- I know I am really good at
  ....

- I feel really good after I
  ....

- It might be a good time to
  ....

- I fear I might not
  ....

- I know I am doing what I love because I feel
  ....

Those phrases are clues that you are in a situation that you don't like. It's time to make a plan to get into a better situation. If you are in a work environment that is only temporary and you don't like it, make a plan for better. I have seen people working in a job out of desperation, as many of us might be forced to do due to childcare requirements, family issues, or insurance needs. We do what is necessary for the good of our families, even though it might not be by design and certainly might not be the best choice. When you are in a situation like this, it's important to think about what you can do to improve it.

A friend of mine accepted a job in his uncle's packaging business because he had been laid off and needed an income to support his family. He despised the job and hoped to find a new job relatively soon. But when he realized he was not as marketable as he had thought, he resigned himself to staying in a job that he hated. This took a toll on his marriage and strained his relationship with his uncle, who had only been trying to help him out. What my friend didn't realize was how he was wasting his "free time." Instead of thinking about the future and planning, he worked day after day, complaining and frustrated. He could have been taking classes and changed career directions to get him into a different job that he loved. Six years later, he is again laid off, and has not acquired any new skills.

Readers, you deserve to be happy and to feel successful in whatever job you love to do. But how can you feel it when you take no imitative to find it? Let your guard down, ask for help, seek guidance, and pursue a better life. Take classes, even just one at a time, knowing that eventually you will reach your goal. Any and all education in your field of choice can only get you closer to the work of your dreams.

What's *not* good is wasting time. Time moves on and if you don't put a stake in the ground and claim your work goals and begin to pursue them, you will often find yourself still in the same place years down the road. Please, ask yourself, are you doing what you love?

A Mental Health Note

As you begin your journey with this book, I'll remind you to check your mental health, since depression, anxiety, and other acute issues can hold us back in ways we can't understand. For many people who suffer with mental health issues, getting help in the form of therapy, medications, and other holistic treatments can be life-transforming. Some folks have a biological chemical imbalance such that no matter what they do, they just can't seem to shake the blues. Take the time to see a mental health professional or your primary care physician if you have concerns.

Sometimes having your concerns heard makes all the difference between thinking negatively about your dreams and actually achieving them with confidence. Give that great gift to yourself of growth and deep happiness, and get a wonderful therapist! It's okay to reach out for help, and therapists are trained to help you sort your feelings out. Your friends may offer guidance and support, but a trained therapist can identify mental health concerns and begin the process of improvement with you. It is emotionally freeing to heal past wounds or learn new coping strategies for managing depression or other mental health concerns. Depression takes a toll on you physically and emotionally, making it feel impossible to welcome new ideas and exciting goals. Please know that help is out there; I encourage you to embrace it!

• •

"When it comes to making a big change in your life, you have to want it more than you fear it." – Unknown

• •

2

Make the time for play.

Where Do I Spend My Time?

n this chapter, we'll tackle an important and very big question: Where do you spend your time? So often when I discuss with my clients the idea of living a fulfilling life, the phrase "not enough time" gets thrown out at some point, if not repeated constantly. My hope is that everyone has enough time to **play, rest, reflect, refresh, laugh, and daydream.** And by "everyone," I mean *you*!

If you are laughing at that, saying "yeah, right," you may be someone who *really* needs to answer this question about where you spend your time. It's no joke. How can other people, who are just as busy as, if not busier than you, still make the time to play and have "me time," but you can't? It's all in who or what is taking your time and how well you manage the time that you have. I won't give you a lecture on time management, but I will share this piece of advice with you. Instead of *wishing* you had more time for the fun things you would like to do, start *making* the time. Then the next step is to be sure you do something with the free time you finally have.

Make the time for play.

Actually play in the free time you made.

The thought of waiting to have free time once the kids go back to school or once you are retired and can make your own schedule is very enticing. Wouldn't it be nice to have more "you" time, fewer schedules and structured time? Of course it would! But if you don't have a plan, then free time just becomes empty time. Truth be told, this also leads directly to depression and boredom. You have to make *good* use of your time. Simply having plenty of time doesn't make you a happier person; you must keep investing that time wisely to get to the place you want to be.

What are you doing to keep yourself actively participating in your own self-growth? If you are tired and annoyed when the kids leave for school and then you spend every day cleaning and doing chores, when the kids come home you are still just as tired and annoyed. If before you retire you have no hobbies or social circle, you may find the free time lonely and depressing. Start now to invest in yourself. Make yourself a better person for *you*! Your future self will thank you for it, I promise you!

How will you design your life if you feel you never have a free moment to even think about it? It's no surprise that you would not be so happy, running from place to place, person to person, feeling that there is never time for you to create your life as you want it. Are you waiting for someone else to find the time for you? Stop waiting, and let's get started!

Time Pie Exercise

Grab a piece of paper, and draw a large circle on it and divide that circle up like a pie, creating a "slice" for each activity that represents how you spend your time. After you've done this and labeled each slice, notice how you divided up your "time pie." Is half the pie work and the other half obligations? Is there even a slim slice of fun in there? Now turn the paper over, and draw the circle again, this time dividing up the pie to represent the way you would *like* your life to be. Now compare the two "time pies." The first drawing you did shows you how your life is today, while the second drawing represents how you would like it to be. Are the two drawings the same? If they are, good for you! You are in control of your time!

If they are not the same, is there a way to add more of what you want in your life? It doesn't have to mean making big, major changes at this time, but making some changes, even smaller ones, can have a dramatic impact on your life.

If you say to yourself, "well, someday I will have more time," you defeat the purpose of this book. Remember, the title is *The Right Time Is Right Now!* "Now" meaning "right now," as you hold this book in your hand. Why wait? Will you ever truly have free time?

••••••••••••••••••••••••••••••••••••••

If you don't start working towards the life you want, time passes and you will still find yourself feeling just as you do right now, only it will be five years later, then ten years later, and your same self will show up, still lacking time, still trying to figure out what is missing.

••••••••••••••••••••••••••••••••••••••

Why wait? Start now! Ask yourself these questions:

- Who takes up all your time?

  ....

- What takes up all your time?

  ....

  ....

- Do you have enough time?

  ....

- When you have free time, who or what gets it?

- Who would like more of it?

When it comes to *your* time, the precious time that you need to guard for yourself so that you can create the life you want, you must first envision it, and that takes time. Here is a simple phrase to help get you more time for yourself: *Set better boundaries.* Get in the habit of simply saying *no*.

It's helpful to evaluate where your time is spent, connecting it to your most active time of day. If you do your best work in the morning, wake up early and get to it! You might like to work out in the morning, then complete the day's hardest tasks so when the afternoon comes around, you're feeling successful and complete. On the contrary, if nighttime is your best time to accomplish things, don't squander that "you time" by sitting in front of the television or computer for hours. Instead, do something that makes you a better person!

- If I had more time I would

- I wish I could say no to

- If I could cut out one activity from my life, it would be

- I would like to add these activities to my life

....

....

- If I spend less time doing _____, then I will have more time to do

....

....

Stop Wasting Your Energy

Many of us focus our energy on the wrong stuff. We waste our precious energy, squandering it day after day, until we end up with nothing left. Free up your mind from constant worry, because worry replaces positive thoughts with fear and anxiety. Thinking about your fat butt all day will not make your butt any smaller; it simply makes you feel angry, frustrated, and bad about yourself. That's not time well spent. Time well spent is actually going to the gym or going for a walk. If you are doing your best, believe it is your best and stop wasting your energy thinking about it all day long, and let it go.

Our thoughts can stress us out and use up all of our energy in nonproductive ways. For example, do you find yourself thinking: Am I good enough? Am I doing enough, what should I be doing? More? Less? Did I choose the right path or the wrong one? Please be kind and patient with yourself. Don't second-guess all your choices. If you have made them already, what's done is done, so move forward. Don't waste all that good energy on stuff you can't change! What's your priority right now? Changing the past? We all know you can't do that!

Before you can create the life you want, it's important to determine who and what is getting your time and energy now.

Delegate

You can't do everything, so don't even try. Instead, ask those around you for help and actually allow them to do it. Being the go-to, know-it-all, do-it-all person will not earn you any free time; in fact, it will rob you of any free time. When people offer to help you, take them up on it and delegate your tasks when you can. Let go of the desire to be the only one to do certain tasks because you want them done "right." If they are done well (or even done at all), that should be good enough. I hear this excuse all the time: "I'm the only one who does it right," referring but not limited to household and yard chores, child rearing, work responsibilities, and social events planning. Please learn to delegate.

Be Consistent

Your time is precious and limited. In order to develop new patterns that serve you better, you must be consistent and practice them as often as possible so that they become habits that help you form a new way of life. Don't just take time out for yourself once a month; make it daily, weekly, a way of life. If you say no, say it consistently so people know you mean business. Don't waver. Once you're in the habit of going out to do an activity, you will get used to doing so and it will become part of your life. The ultimate goal is creating time for fun, activities, and enjoyment that all become a regular part of your life, not just a once-in-a-while event.

By the way, you will notice a difference in those around you when you subscribe to a way of life in which you have clearly defined boundaries for your "fun time." Others will learn to respect your time and appreciate that these activities are part of your lifestyle, rather just something you do "when you have time." When you participate in activities at random, the people in your life will assume these activities don't matter since you do them so rarely, and they expect you to cancel your plans to assist them in theirs. They will expect this and you will cancel, and then you'll find yourself saying, "See, I don't have the time for fun." Please be mindful of others' expectations about your time, and be consistent with your own habits around play.

Self-Discipline

It's time to ask yourself again, where do I spend my time?

- If I do find myself with free time, do I waste it on non-essential activities and in non-essential places?
- Do I frequently say to myself, "I thought I had more time and now I am rushing"?
- Can I set time limits on my computer use so all my free time isn't spent sucked into other people's lives on Facebook?
- Can I get rid of the mindset that free time is meant for doing *something*, including chores, household projects, and other people's projects? Something isn't always better than nothing. When it comes to your time, doing nothing can be

just as rewarding. What about slowing down, relaxing, putting your feet up and watching the stars?

Do you possess the self-discipline to use your free time wisely? Some of us naturally adopt a hurried, fast pace of life and we forget how nice it feels to slow it all down when the opportunity arises. If you are lucky enough to have a nice summer home near the ocean or on a lake, you know how great it feels to put your hurried life aside for the weekend or a week and breathe in relaxation. For those of us who don't have that in our lives, how can we create that same feeling in our backyards or in our homes?

My best friend Julie can often be heard giving this advice to others: "If you want something bad enough, you have to make the time." She knows very well to be self-disciplined in her time and her use of it. Her story is an inspiring one — she went back to nursing school after years of being out of school, working full-time and managing a family with two young children. Her aha moment came when she was overlooked for a supervisory position; despite years of experience she was not going to move up the career ladder without an advanced degree. Her choices were to do nothing and complain, or to go back to school. The ultimate question was, how badly did she want to advance and get her dream job? Did she want this badly enough to turn her world upside down for two years? Going back to school required a commitment on her part, but more importantly, it required her time. She had to delegate chores to family members and take any existing free time and devote it to studying and schoolwork. Not easy, but not impossible.

Two years have since passed and she reflects back on it with pride. She was incredibly self-disciplined with her time and energy in pursuit of a job she would one day love. She now has a job she loves with better pay and benefits, and is overall a more rewarding experience. She is quick to encourage people of all ages who also want to pursue their goal of going back to school to not dismiss it so quickly as "impossible, too difficult, no time." It *is* possible. She did it. So can you.

Guilt, Self-Centered and Other "Bad Words"

"I can't take time out for me because I feel guilty."

"If I have too much fun, I feel like I'm being selfish."

Does this sound like you? Whether you feel guilty because taking a day off from work might make the place implode or your kid tantrums when you leave, guilt will keep you exactly where you don't want to be, stuck pleasing everyone else. They will all get what they want — whether it's your demanding boss, your child or your spouse — and you will get nothing fun. You are not alone in these thoughts and feelings. Many people struggle with guilt. In all the seminars that I give, both the professional lectures on "Job Stress, Burnout and Self-Care" or my women's getaway "Joy Weekend," guilt always comes up as a number one factor in why people are not out there enjoying themselves more.

I have heard of countless vacation days that go unused for fear that problems will arise at work when people leave on vacation. Or the baby won't go to sleep without a certain parent reading to them before bed. You know what? The other parent can figure it out, just like your colleagues can work through any issue while you are gone. Don't let guilt trap you. Don't let your in-laws, children, job colleagues, or spouse pour on the guilt. There is a delicate balance with self-care, one that says, "I give to everyone around me and therefore I give to myself." Living that way is not being selfish or self-centered, it's what you need for survival. You need healthy boundaries in your relationships, work, and personal life to create a guilt-free lifestyle. Be able to say:

- This is my work time and this is my personal time.
- My benefits are there to benefit me when I need a vacation or a personal day.
- A good babysitter will allow me some freedom to enjoy hobbies that I love.

Don't let work take all of your energy; take time off without the guilt. Your spouse's needs shouldn't completely dictate your free time if you need some alone time. Let the guilt go, you are way beyond that. Do it now, take that vacation, enjoy a personal day, get that babysitter so you can go to Zumba class, book that kid-free weekend with your spouse, because *The Right Time Is Right Now!*

Unplug

Do you spend every moment with your phone two inches from your face? Is your time spent connected, plugged in, always in the know on every current event worldwide? Is that you? I see too many people for whom that seems to be the norm, and we've all seen people driving and texting. When can we shut it down for a minute or two or three?

Unplug, ditch your phone, enjoy the moment, take in the sights, and enjoy the conversation. Otherwise, life will pass you by and you will never get that time back.

What does your inner voice want? Can you hear it? When was the last time you not only heard it, but listened to it? Can you have more "unplugged" time? More time connected with those you love? You will hear your inner voice when you are still. The more you hear it, the harder it will get to ignore. You will be called to action, called to align yourself with your true purpose. If you haven't heard your inner voice in a while pointing you in the right direction in your life, reevaluate where and how you spend your time.

Unplug from all the devices and the information that holds you captive. Day after day, we are being fed information from every direction, forcing our minds to take it in, process it, and think about it. When this happens constantly, there is little room in your mind for your own thoughts, ideas, and daydreams. Please consider having times throughout your day or week when you can unplug. If you don't need to take the phone to the dinner table or on an outing, leave it behind. You will only feel forced to check it because it is habit for all of us. We think, if it's here, why not be on it? Instead, leave it behind when you can. How about now? Now is a good time.

Soothing Balm for Your Soul — Do You Know Your Place?

Have you found that place where you can go to soothe your soul? A quiet place that calls to you and only you? Maybe no one knows where you escape to for a little bit of time. We all need that place. For some of us it can be a walk in the woods or by the ocean, or on your own porch or in the comfy chair in the bookstore.

How empowering it is to have a place that grounds you and comforts you, especially when your world can be harsh and demanding. To be alone with your thoughts and cast out your intentions for the week or the year, or maybe just a simple prayer, "Bless me, guide me, show me the way."

Often times, our homes, which are supposed to be our places of refuge, can feel like the opposite of calm and peaceful. Grumpy, overworked spouses and demanding, overbooked children plus loads of laundry and dishes don't exactly say, "Welcome home, sit down and relax." The welcome mat by your front door might say "welcome home," but some of us sometimes wish it would say, "please go away, I can't deal with anyone else today."

If you can't feel the comfort and relaxation in your home, try seeking it elsewhere — the local woods, out in your garden, coffee on your porch while everyone is still sleeping. Those moments will nourish you and bring you back to a place of joy and love. Love for your life and yourself. Isn't that where you have to start anyway, before you can accomplish anything or give to anyone else? Confidence, self-esteem, and self-worth must be worked on and focused on, because you need to have these before you can give love to other people.

A lack of those critical pieces in your life can lead to failed relationships (both friendships and romantic relationships), bad habits that destroy your health, and more stress than you can handle. Self-care is exactly what it says — it's caring for yourself. All the parts of yourself, emotional, physical, mental and spiritual.

When you find that place in your life that can offer comfort and healing balm for the dark, hurt places, you are moving in the right direction. It is often in those quiet moments in those places you love so much that moments of revelation come to you. You begin to figure it all out. The answers come to you.

Go find that place that speaks to your soul. You will know it when you find it. If you are lucky enough to have that place, spend as much time as possible there. It will bless you in more ways that you ever thought possible.

Want Time to Just Be You

So many of us have spent our lives surviving, not thriving. We were programmed at an early age to just get through the day, the months, and the years. It may not have even been in your thoughts to take care of yourself along the way, and as a result much of this talk about self-care can sound foreign and hard to grasp. If you didn't grow up in a family that valued or promoted self-care, it's hard to imagine putting it into your life without feeling guilty or selfish. Since all my workshops include a self-care piece, I not only lecture about it, I take my own advice.

Let me remind you of how necessary it is to carve out time just to be yourself, whatever that may mean for you. People in your life may not think your self-care is a priority, but don't fall into that trap. There is plenty of care to go around, but only if you take care of yourself first.

Make self-care a priority in your daily life, enough to move other commitments out and yourself in!

When you are feeling good, you have enough to share with others. The reverse is also true. If you are drained, exhausted and irritable, how can you take care of anyone else in your life? How can you plan to take care of yourself today?

* *

"I'm working toward a time when everything gives me joy."
—Maya Angelou

* *

3

Friendship is nourishment for your soul.

Do I Have Supportive People in My Social Circle?

W e all need support and true friendship in our lives, as friendship is nourishment for the soul. In fact, not having the support of those around us is often the biggest obstacle to achieving our goals and dreams. Negative comments from negative people can keep us at a standstill. However, having friends, confidants, mentors or business partners with a positive, bright attitude can not only get us moving but also keep us moving when we need it most. This chapter helps you to examine how supportive your social circle is, and encourages you to ask for help and support.

Ask yourself these questions:

- Who are the people closest to me?
- Who do I spend the most time with?
- When I think about the people who surround me on a daily basis, what thoughts come to mind?

Keeping in mind your answers to the questions above, ask yourself, do you have a large social circle or a few great friends? Do you know who to share good news with and who *not* to share your good news with? It may be hard to believe, but not having the support of those around you often can be the biggest obstacle to achieving your goals and dreams. Negative comments from negative people can keep you stopped dead in your tracks. Fearful people can infect us with that same disease and we become paralyzed and unable to welcome new ideas.

On the brighter side, having a positive person with a can-do attitude as your friend, confidant, mentor or business partner can get you moving and *keep* you moving when you need it most. If you need help and support, *ask for it*. Just ask! Tell your friends and family that you are embarking on a new project, adventure, or goal, and that you need their support to help keep you moving in the right direction. Ask to be guided or to be mentored by those who you admire. Meet with them, ask them how they did it, and see what you can learn from them.

I am thrilled to tell you there is actual research on this important issue! In his book *The Happiness Advantage*, Shawn Achor writes:

> *"In my research, I've found that positive social connection is the greatest predictor of long-term happiness. Welcoming a positive new influencer into your world can be one of the most important choices of happiness you make. That person might be a professional life coach, or a mentor or simply someone whom you respect and who has the positive outlook you want to emulate."*

Wow! Let's repeat part of Shawn's quote one more time: "Welcoming a positive new influencer into your world can be one of the most important choices of happiness you make." Sit with that thought. Do you realize the power of influence your social group has? They can uplift or deflate your thoughts, feelings, ideas, dreams, and goals...all of it.

As adults, we can sometimes find it hard to enlarge our social circle, and my clients often ask me how they might do just that. Do these remarks sound like you? "It feels weird to try to meet friends at this age." "I don't know where to begin."

Where can you make new connections? Just about anywhere! It's perfectly fine to reach out to someone you see every day at the gym, people you speak with at religious gatherings, or the moms and dads at your kids' sporting events or school. *Reach out.* Introduce yourself. Invite friends over to watch sports games. Gather a group of friends to see a new movie. Host a board game night for adults. Have a campfire in your yard and invite your neighbors. Allow new people and new energy into your life. Be open to people with new ideas and open to fun experiences.

Let me make a very important point. If you have children who are very involved in school or community activities, or you are very involved in many hobbies and still do not have any meaningful friendships, please check your self-esteem and self-confidence. The lack of friendships might have more to do with you than with others. Keep reading, I'll explain in the next section below.

How do you present yourself to the public?

Think about how you appear to others. Do you seem closed off, unhappy, or glowing?

If you seem closed off, here's how you appear to others: Not making eye contact, not interested in conversation. Result: People will read you as "closed off" and not approach you.

If you seem unhappy, here's how you appear to others: Scowl on your face, not smiling, always complaining. Result: People will do *anything* to avoid getting stuck next to you, because life is hard enough, and who needs people who will make you feel worse?

If you seem to be glowing, here's how you appear to others: Smiling, happy, joyful, and confident. Result: Everyone wants to talk with you and be with you.

Now think about someone who is sulking, unhappy, and complaining to anyone who will listen, and someone else who is smiling, positive, and present.

Which person would you prefer to be with?

Like attracts like.

....
As Rumi once said, "Be with those who help your being."
....

Surround yourself with caring, loving people who are your cheerleaders to keep you moving in the right direction and act as your confidants when you need solid advice. If you have your head down as if you are unsure of yourself, who will you attract? Not those who feel empowered and confident, strong, and assured of themselves. What do you value in others? What do you want to attract? Are you smiling or frowning? If you are insecure, it may be difficult to meet new friends for fear they may judge you or you may not be good enough. Rest assured, you are plenty good enough; find the courage and ditch the fear.

Are you a reflection of the friends you keep? Or do you tell people, "please don't judge me by my friends"? Your friends have a big influence on you! That's why I dedicated a whole chapter to them. Don't underestimate the importance of your social group to your decisions and your self-esteem. Do the people in your social circle uplift or deflate you?

The wrong people can have devastating consequences on your life.
Whether it be a spouse, lover, friend, cousin or neighbor, negative people can have
a dramatic effect on how we see the world. Sometimes we don't even realize it until we experience a positive person and realize how refreshing and soothing they
are to be with. Then we think, wow, so that's how it feels to be loved and supported
unconditionally. Guilt can also play a factor in why negative people are still part
of our circle despite the toxic energy they bring with them. Stop feeling guilty.
Allowing yourself to stay in a negative relationship because of guilt will only bring
you down further, because now you have guilt *and* resentment towards that person. You are resenting them for holding you hostage in an unfulfilling friendship
or relationship. Free yourself from guilt and resentment. Let it go, and go after the
uplifting and inspiring people.

Kate married young and spent nineteen years with the man she once thought
was the man of her dreams. They had similar values and had two children. As the
children got involved in their own activities, more friendships came to them. Kate
was very social and welcomed all the new friendships and the fun that came with
them. Her job was not particularly rewarding because they had recently moved
and she had taken anything just to make some money, with the hope of changing
jobs at some point. She noticed that her husband wasn't interested in joining her
at any social activities and had a negative word for her and their life together at all
times. Seen through his eyes, the world was gloom and unhappiness. He found
fault with everything. Kate found this becoming more and more exhausting and
unbearable. When it came to trying new things, she never had his blessing or his

support, so she simply didn't try them. At times, she even found herself buying into his gloomy, pessimistic outlook on life.

Kate tried her best, but after many years of living in his negative world, she took a very hard and challenging road and decided to divorce. She had no idea what the negativity had done to her life until afterward. Without that gloom in her life, she saw the world anew. She fully engaged in all the social activities with more confidence and joy, and she soon began dating someone with similar interests. She found a new job and began working out again. She felt like a new person. The decision to divorce was not an easy one and did not come to her overnight. It had taken years of thinking, praying, and trying to make it work. When she closed a chapter in her life that was bringing her down, she opened a new chapter that brought the sunshine in! What a difference it has made for both her and her children!

Let me remind you one more time,

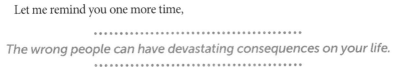

The wrong people can have devastating consequences on your life.

I realize this type of change, divorce in particular, is a very difficult situation, and might be the extreme version of changing your social circle. I do recommend speaking with a therapist trained in relationship issues as they can provide the support, guidance and insight needed to help you make these life changes.

An example from Erin's life, one less difficult than Kate's, sheds light on how we can get into a trap with the best of intentions. Erin admits that she initially invited people over each summer because she preferred being in her own yard and having her friends enjoy it too. She had a beautiful in-ground swimming pool and everything and anything you would need to enjoy a beautiful summer weekend. "Each weekend the same people would come over with their kids, enjoy our food and drinks and we thought it was fine." Towards the end of the summer, she had an "aha moment" after hearing them gossip and complain about other people. "I realized I didn't even like them! I no longer enjoyed their company and we figured out that we were spending $200 a weekend on food and drinks, which our friends never reciprocated." Erin admitted, "We just got into this routine of the same people we have known for years coming over each weekend, thinking nothing of it, until we sat back and discovered we didn't want this anymore."

The way out was not too difficult: "It didn't become a big deal, we just told everyone we were going on vacation and we would be in touch when we got back, and then we never did." This story reminds me of that great quote that applies to everyone at some point in their life, from selfhelpdaily.com:

> *What you allow is what will continue.*

Take a moment to think about your social patterns in your life.

- What type of person do you attract?

- Who comes into your life?

- Who have you not let in?

- Do you take the risk of introducing yourself?

- Are all your friends people who other friends have introduced you to?

- Or do you make quality friends on your own?

- What is your pattern for meeting new people?

- Is it easy to meet new people?   ☐ yes   ☐ no

- If it's hard for you to meet new people, why?

- Do you walk around with your head down or your eyes glued to your phone?

When you open a conversation with a smile on your face and a readiness to embrace new people, you will meet new friends. If you are hiding in the corner hoping no one will notice you, let alone speak to you, that's where you end up. Alone in the corner. Now how can that be helpful to your life? We all need support and true friendship in our lives. Don't fool yourself, you are not excluded from this!

Friendship is nourishment for your soul. We all yearn for some type of connection with people. Some of us prefer large groups of friends and others a few strong friendships; either way, connection is at the heart of each of us. We want to feel connected and no one wants to feel excluded from the group. Through tears, joys, new beginnings and hard endings, connection with the right people will see us through. Whether you have something exciting to share or your sorrow is too much to bear, the power of a good friend can be just what you need. If you are going without, it's time to change.

Focus on your self-esteem. Remember what I said in Chapter 1 about mental and emotional health. Do you have issues in your life that you need help with, but can never find the time to really work on them? Are they holding you back from fully engaging with other people? Take care of those issues now. It could be a long journey, but start now because it's worth it. Having friends who love you and laugh with you is sometimes the best medicine of all! You deserve amazing company by your side! You've seen all the sayings about friendship in the greeting card stores:

YOUR friendship KEEPS ME GOING DAY AFTER DAY.

YOU WILL ALWAYS BE my friend YOU KNOW TOO MUCH!

My friends HAVE MADE THE STORY OF MY LIFE.

It's because it's all true! There are cards, movies, television shows, and songs about friendship and how healing it is to be surrounded by true and loving friends. Friendships can take work, because life gets in the way, and other priorities come up and time gets away from us. It takes phone calls, scheduled get-togethers (which might get canceled and rescheduled three times before they actually happen), and the desire for two people to want to stay connected. If it is one-sided, it doesn't work. Put the requisite effort into your friendships, make the phone calls, and stay diligent about the scheduled get-togethers. It is through that effort that friendships stay strong and current.

Welcome a positive influencer into your life today. The benefits are limitless. The right time is right now.

- I wish I had
- The two biggest supporters in my life are
- When I need advice, I speak with
- When I want to share my joys, I tell
- My social circle is big enough: ☐ yes   ☐ no
- I need more positive people in my life: ☐ yes   ☐ no

- If I need positive reinforcement, I ask

- I have friends to share my burdens and fears ☐ yes ☐ no

- I need to work on expanding my social circle ☐ yes ☐ no

- If yes, how will you?

Besides surrounding myself with positive people, do I surround myself with positive messages?

Even though this chapter focuses on friendships and the power of positive influencers in our lives, I want to quickly touch upon what surrounds our everyday lives and how that can also make a difference. Are you tuned in to all the news every day, absorbing the negative, fear-based messages sent to you via television, internet or radio? Are you reading all the gossip magazines that spread lies, betrayal and sadness? What about reality television, where anger, violence and nastiness become the norm? How about taking a break from it all? Try filling your days with more positive, inspiring messages that uplift and refresh. Try music or books that bring out the best in you, not the worst. Self-help books can be powerful tools for self-improvement and success. Try falling asleep at night to peaceful music instead of a loud, obnoxious television show. Go to sleep in peace, not filled with angst over who just betrayed who on a nasty television show. Displaying positive messages around your office and your home can brighten your spirits.

Did you know you can unfollow your Facebook friends, and better yet, if you are that disgusted by them, you can unfriend them? It just takes a click of your finger and you no longer need to be annoyed by their posts. It's easy to do and I highly recommend it. If you find yourself becoming annoyed, angry, and offended by certain people's posts, comments, and pictures on social media, hit the delete button and be done. So much negativity takes a toll on us. Better to use social media to make yourself feel good, not annoyed.

I know this sounds very elementary, but trust me, if you are looking at positive messages and getting peaceful vibes from your radio, it can put you in the right frame of mind to continue with a successful journey. To the contrary, if every day you are stuck in nasty news, gossip on Facebook, and violent television shows, how does that prepare you for success? How do those messages give you the courage and the excitement to be your best? For most people, they don't. All they do is reinforce the negative mindset that stepping out of your comfort zone could be dangerous, and not well received by others. Don't give in to that ideology. If you need a break, try stepping away from all those messages and replace them with positive ones.

Distractions are everywhere, often closer than we think.

Distractions come in the form of television, the computer, noise, and most hurtful, people you know and trust. Some of these people are acquaintances, others are those we thought were good friends and family members. They are all around us, causing us to lose our focus and bringing us to a place of frustration and hurt.

It only takes a few ignorant people to cause you to lose your forward momentum. Comments made on Facebook can bring you to your knees in pain. Gossip causes your mind to be filled with anger or annoyance, and soon enough the positive energy you need to accomplish your goals is long gone. The positive feelings are replaced with negative ones. You can't see straight. "How could she say that?" you wail. Or filled with rage, you shout, "Why is he writing about that?"

These people know exactly what they are doing. They are consumed with jealously and envy as they watch you, the strong one, accomplish your goals, enjoy amazing friends, and genuinely live your life with joy. They are serving as your distractions. How mentally strong can you be to avoid getting sucked into the negativity? They are testing your limits; will you respond with a nasty email? Will you give in and let go of your successes to be low with them?

Don't do it, I beg of you. Let it all go. Show me your strength in letting it all go. They can't take it, it strikes a chord within them, one that has a collection of past and present hurt, low self-esteem and low energy for moving in the right direction. They haven't done the work, and they want to sit back and have your life, yet they don't want to work for it.

Ask yourself, what does friendship with these negative people bring you? Is it more beneficial for them than for you? You are the giver, the one who would like to see them better themselves, but they are full of too many excuses. But you blew all your excuses out of the water when you put that first goal into motion, owning it all.

Please don't shrink down to those distractions. These people are not real friends; they are simply distractions to your success. Don't apologize for being happy. Don't give in to it and meet them on their negative energy vibration. Don't do it.

Rise above it. Stay strong. Quietly bless them that they might have the courage to achieve their own success one day. Then walk away from it. They haven't seen your quiet tears of perseverance, your sadness when plans have changed again in accomplishing your dreams or the tiredness of holding up your world and making time to achieve your own goals. Don't get fooled by those hurtful comments that can come at you like daggers through your heart. You let them in a little and they take more than they give. Never asking about you, only making snide comments on why is it that you "get to have it all."

When you work hard for it, never giving up, always pushing to be your personal best, you deserve to shine.

Travel with your friends. Go often and with joy in your heart. Buy yourself nice clothes if that pleases you. Enjoy the financial freedom you have earned to buy and do what you want when you want. Sit with the joy that comes from knowing you are creating your life exactly how you want it to be. You have earned the right to bask in the glow. *Shine bright!*

"My friends have made the story of my life."

4

Planning your fun is the key
to making it actually happen!

Do I Regularly Participate in Activities that Bring Me Joy?

Now that you've thought about the state of the friendships and relationships in your life, let me ask you to reflect on whether you have favorite activities you regularly participate in. Everyone needs to enjoy themselves — life is no fun if it's all work and no play.

Before you answer this question, note the word "regularly." By "regularly," I don't mean once every month or twice per year. I'm asking whether you have enjoyable activities that you participate in once a week, if not more than that. I should mention one more important thought before we continue. Just so I have your attention, *no one is exempt!* Not one person is exempt from enjoying themselves. Adults sometimes feel that the kids are allowed to have the fun and the grown-ups are just supposed to work and make sure everyone else is having a great time. What fun is life when it becomes all work and no play? When chores become all that is involved, life gets dull, monotonous, and almost burdensome. Very little fulfillment comes from the daily grind. Here are some adjectives that describe how you can feel as the direct result of engaging in activities you love:

Happy	Joyful
Fulfilled	Excited
Challenged	Good
Great	Awesome
Successful	Thrilled
Amazing	Nourished

Wouldn't it be nice to feel those feelings on a *regular* basis?

So back to our original question: Do you regularly participate in activities that bring you joy? If not, why not? What's stopping you? I might not be able to include enough pages in this book for you to write down all your reasons. Does it sometimes feel like a fight just to get fulfilled? Or maybe not even a fight, because you've just forgotten or given up and it feels like it would take too much energy to get moving again? Especially if you are not even sure what you enjoy anymore. Or if coordinating babysitting and friends' schedules seems impossible, you resign yourself to "another time." The problem with that thinking is that another time never comes. As grown-ups, we have to be diligent about including fun time in our lives. The way to make this happen is to make sure activities, friends, and hobbies are planned into our schedules. If these things are not planned, we can all too easily get into the mindset that there is something better to do, and it's usually not what will fulfill us. Planning your fun is the key to making it actually happen! It's worth the effort! I see so many people who wear their exhaustion or burnout like a banner across their weary head, saying things like:

- "I'm tired."
- "I'm living to shuttle my kids around."
- "All I do is work."
- "Maybe I can have fun when I'm retired."
- "I can't remember the last time I had fun."
- "I never do anything fun."
- "Fun, what's fun?"

What do *you* find fun? Not an activity that someone else finds fun, but something that makes *you* happy while you are doing it. You need the fun activities to brighten your spirit and your heart. Where does *your* fulfillment come from? When you are doing something you love, *you are not stressed*, but instead you are focused and enjoying. When you are feeling tired and out of energy, this is your slogan:

You need to infuse the positive, exciting energy back into your body and spirit to help you get through your daily life. This is where most people get it wrong. They think if they take time out to have fun, they will be more stressed by all the things they weren't doing and there will be more work for them when they return. They worry that taking a vacation means they will come back to work with more work to do. They believe that if they go out for fun instead of staying home to do housework, the chores will pile up more. What a way to live! Does it make sense to never enjoy anything because something else is always waiting to stress you out more? You will have more energy to tackle the "must do" items once you take time away to do something you love! Wear this banner instead:

Take a moment to answer these questions, either writing down your answers or simply thinking them through.

- If I had more time, I would

- The last time I felt fulfilled was
  because I was doing

- The hobbies that bring me joy are

- The last time I participated in hobbies that bring me joy was:
  ☐ last week   ☐ last month   ☐ last year   ☐ more than a year ago

- I would like to regularly participate in

- If I had one free night a week, I would

- If I had more time on the weekends, I would

- The last time I felt overwhelmed with happiness was when I was

- The last vacation I took was (date)

- When is my next vacation? Am I going to be using it to do something that I enjoy?

If you found your answers to the questions about "when" and "how often" to be "a long time ago" or "not enough," it's time to put that fun back into your life. You don't need to have a ton of money to do what you love. Start by carving out time (refer back to Chapter 2 and Question 2 if you need help in that area), and add one fun activity. I can't do it for you, because I don't know what you like to do. You know what is fun for you and what is not enjoyable. I find that as people age, the message from our inner voice about what we don't enjoy comes through louder and clearer. That's a good thing — we develop more insight and don't want to waste time on non-fulfilling activities. Now that you know what you *don't* want to do…what *do* you want to do?

"Just be you." You have heard this a million times, but it's true. What brings you joy might be very different from your family's or friend's choices. Everyone is different and has unique tastes. Your journey will be different from everyone else's. Embrace that, and stop worrying what others will think if you participate in activities that you love. You just need to work at being the best version of you. Don't try hard to "fit in" when you know you don't. That will be your biggest mistake yet. If you enjoy running, then go run, but if you don't enjoy running races, then don't let your friend convince you to run them. If you love to go away to the mountains, then don't let your spouse convince you that you *really* like New York City. We all compromise, and I'm sure you have done your share of compromising. That's okay, as long as you get your needs met, too, and you don't compromise your free time so that it is really someone else's free time.

> *Stop worrying what others will think if you*
> *participate in activities that you love.*

If you are struggling to meet new people, make the time to visit places that interest you, participate in activities you love, and reach out, make eye contact and say hello. That's how you meet new, interesting people. You don't meet them with your eyes glued to your phone, or sitting alone on your couch. Fully participating in your life means taking chances, meeting new people, and trying new activities. Open yourself up to adventure — you won't regret it!

Do more of what makes you awesome.

This is especially important when other parts of your life aren't going so well. This is when hobbies make a big difference. They can take you away for just a little bit, make you feel a little less stressed and a lot more fulfilled. They remind you that there is fun to be had, that you are good at something, even when you feel like all is not headed in a good direction. The positive charge you get when you engage in what you love affects your body, mind and spirit. It's like an electric charge of joy goes right to your soul. When you have challenges in your life, it's nice to know you can step out for a little bit each day or each week into another, happier place. I love to hear remarks like these:

- "I love to go out for a run every morning, it gives me the upbeat feeling I need."
- "I need yoga to balance my life — without it I would be a mess."
- "If I didn't bowl every Thursday with my best friends, my week would be ruined."
- "Scrapbooking allows me to be creative and take my mind off things for a while. "
- "If I couldn't ski every weekend in the winter, I would be so depressed! I love to ski!"
- "Massage relaxes and nourishes me, I would hate to be without it!"

Men are not excluded from this either! Men can let go of their hobbies just as easily as women can, especially if they are working longer hours to support the home, the kids, and the general expenses of life. It often takes a toll on everyone when parents no longer find fun in their own lives, where work is the majority and play is in the minority — the happiness level is down and out. Although it's admirable when men sacrifice for their family, they must also engage in hobbies that they enjoy.

I would always marvel at my hockey friends who laced up their skates at 10 on a Sunday night after a long day of coaching hockey games and practices. Some of them worked weekends and after they put the kids to bed they would head out to the rink to play. I just couldn't believe they would do it! Now it makes sense to me. Doing something they love to do, despite the undesirable hour, makes them better people; they benefit from having time to do what they love with the camaraderie of friendship and fun. Hockey is not for everyone, so what do you do?

As I mentioned earlier in this chapter, *regularly* participating in fun activities or hobbies is the key word. Can you relate to one of the above? If you can't, use this chapter as a reminder to yourself that you are worthy of having fun in your life. I'm giving you permission to go out and play. Forget your worries for a little while, recharge your brain by doing something you love. Try something different, or go back to something you used to love to do. Dig out those art supplies buried in your attic, grab a new pair of ice skates and find open ice time at your local ice rink. Clean off your camera lens and start taking those pictures you are so good at taking. Lose yourself in nature, find a different trail to hike every weekend. If you are stuck, take a minute to think about what you have heard people tell you are good at. You know, those folks who have actively encouraged you to do something you're good at because they saw you do it in the past. Have you heard comments like these?

"You should go into photography; you take great pictures."
"You would be great singing in a choir, your voice is angelic."
"You would be a great spin teacher; you are the best in the class."
"You are so talented in this…." or "You are a natural at that….."

Have you heard someone make comments like the above to you throughout your lifetime? A teacher perhaps, or maybe a family member, friend or coach? Can you recall something positive they said? If not, and it's something you love, the best part of being an adult is doing it anyway! Even if you are not good at something but you love to do it, go for it. We are hopefully past the stage of "what will they think of me?" and have transitioned confidently to "who cares what people say, I'm doing it because I love how it makes me feel!"

The Giving Up

Call it what you want — sacrifice, letting go temporarily or just plain calling it quits. As adults, we tend to sacrifice for good reason when it comes to letting go of our favorite activities in order to take care of children or other family members, or adapt to a spouse's schedule or our own work schedule. We sacrifice for the good of others, sometimes not realizing that it has become a habit and something that people expect of us.

It's funny that as more time opens up for us, it can seem impossible to put *what once was* back into the schedule. As each month and each year passes, the fun doesn't come back as easily as it was given up. Now's a good time to integrate it back into your life, don't you think? First, decide what it is you want to do, and then figure out a plan to integrate fun back into your life, or at least some semblance of it. If you can't go back to teaching kickboxing, can you at least take a few classes? If you can't be the book club leader, can you attend and enjoy? Move things around, call on help, keep trying.

The Taking Back

Are those fighting words? Is it just easier *not to* integrate the fun and playtime back into your life? You say you'll do it, maybe someday when life is easier and time is plentiful. When is that exactly? The very point of me writing this book is to say to you, *How about now?* Are you ready for some type of fun activity that gives you joy and makes you smile? If you continue waiting, when you finally get to that time, you will be all wrung out, body, mind and spirit, so much so that you might never get off the couch. It will take effort, depending on your life situation, but follow these steps.

1. Put in the effort: Find something you want to do that makes you happy.
2. Persevere: Keep at it, find a way to make it happen; your hard work will pay off.
3. Plan: Get *you* in the schedule, put time for yourself in your schedule.
4. Have fun: Make sure your life includes smiles, laughter, joy, happiness, and fulfillment.

Please keep in mind a few important concepts to help you get to where you want to be.
Don't spend your time hoping everyone else will be okay. How can you go out and enjoy yourself or be relaxed enough to enjoy a night out if you are worrying about everyone else's happiness? There will always be someone who isn't happy, and that is not your problem or responsibility. Let it go, you go out and get happy!

Get excited for change, don't fear it! How can you try new activities or meet new people if you aren't willing to take the risk? All beginnings have a risk, so you need to understand that it will be okay if it doesn't work out. Try anyway.

Here are some common fears and the ways they might limit you:

- I fear planes so I don't travel.
- I fear leaving my kids with a babysitter, so I don't go out alone or with my spouse.
- I fear something bad is going to happen to me, so I don't venture far from home.
- I fear the germs at the gym, so I don't work out.
- I fear the heat so I don't go outside.
- I fear the cold so I stay inside.
- I fear betrayal so I don't get close to people.

Fear looks like this

Joy looks like this

Want it all to happen and happen successfully this instant? Our society has been moving at such a fast pace, we have been conditioned to want everything *now*. Realizing that finding that special hobby or activity might take some time can get you to a better mindset. Just because your friends have told you how amazing spin class is, that doesn't mean you will love it too. Don't get disappointed and give up, just keep moving, and eventually you will find something/someplace that offers just what you need! Think about that feeling you will get when you find something you love to do and then get to do it regularly!

Welcome a New Mindset

If you need to clear out some of that negative energy to make way for a lighter, more positive self, try the increasingly popular alternative therapies, some of which are even covered by health insurance. Yoga, mindfulness, acupuncture, massage, tai chi, and aromatherapy all promote a healthier lifestyle and a calming of the mind that everyone could use a dose of. Be good to yourself and realize when you need extra help to move in the right direction.

Ask yourself the following questions:

- Do I regularly waste my energy on things I can't control, therefore not allowing myself the time and mental energy to do something fun?
- Do I sour my own mood?
- Do I spend a large amount of time worrying?

- Do I obsess over past events/conversations/details that I can no longer control?
- Do I sweat the "small stuff"?

I see so many people who lack simple enjoyment in their lives because worrying takes it away from them. Worrying can keep you closed off and consume all of your mental energy. This is the energy you need in order to even think about doing the fun stuff! You can't have both — you can't be worrying and having fun at the same time! Creative moments will not happen if you are hyper-focused on what you can't control. Let it go. Free your mind and you will feel light and ready to embrace new opportunities. Some women spend so much mental energy on how they look.

- "Am I fat?"
- "Does this make me look thin?"
- "Should I eat this or that? Have I gained five pounds? Should I lose seven pounds?"

The answer is to embrace a healthy lifestyle, eat well, exercise, and take care of your body. Stop stressing about the must-do list associated with this, and integrate small, healthy changes into your everyday life. Stop the fad diets, get rid of the January 1 resolution to lose twenty-five pounds in a month, and start the healthy lifestyle for the long term.

Taking the steps covered in this chapter requires you to have a certain amount of courage as you set out to try new activities and begin new adventures. I am constantly amazed (and saddened) by people who get invited to many of the same activities as I do, yet for some reason they can never seem to get their act together to actually go, whatever their reasons or excuses. I try to take advantage of the fun stuff that is happening around me, whether it be a free concert in the park, a weekend away, a comedy night or a local dance performance. Many of these activities are promoted all over Facebook, and since so many people are on Facebook for so much of their time, there is a good chance that they too can see the same events. After any given activity or event, I hear from those who expressed interest in going but failed to show. "Oh, that looked like fun, I wish I went too." Or, "I have been so busy, I forgot to register."

Sometimes people ask: Should I be spontaneous or plan well in advance?

I encourage both! There are activities that require adequate planning to make them happen, and that's where the Nike slogan comes in handy. *Just do it!* So simple, yet so often not done.

Whether it's a week's vacation, kayak rentals, or free museum passes from the library, you must do a certain amount of planning to make it happen!

There are plenty of opportunities to be spontaneous — a trip to the beach, the movies, or the mall — that require almost no planning at all. Be spontaneous, pick up and break your routine when you can! But know the difference between activities that don't easily lend themselves to last-minute decisions, and those that do. So much passes you by when you leave planning to the last minute. Even with the best intentions, you will come up short.

Be spontaneous, pick up and break your routine when you can!

Every year Jan gets invited to go Nantucket for vacation. Every spring when her parents start planning their vacation, they invite her to bring her two boys along as well. It requires planning — first a commitment to going, and second actually making the reservation. Although her intentions are good, and Jan's children are excited about the possibility of the trip, every year she waits until the last minute to make a reservation and cannot find a place to stay. Every year her children miss out because their mom can't seem to just go ahead and make plans when required.

At the start of every summer, Julie sits with her children and writes out a list of adventures they'd like to have. Some are day trips, others require reservations, and these are offset by day camps to keep the kids busy on the off weeks. This past summer was particularly amazing. They went hiking, biking, and swimming, and saw waterfalls, museums, and the aquarium. All of it happened and all of it was fantastic. Think how this compared to the experiences of friends who would have liked to be doing some of that, but didn't make plans. Sitting back watching TV all summer while the kids make you nuts is not a fun summer for anyone. Don't fall into the same trap when you have a large block of free time available. Don't let "I would love to" turn into "oh well, maybe next year."

Plan it! Do it! Don't miss out!

Get yourself mentally prepared to take on new and challenging activities. Be an active participant in your life, take control of what you are doing. Don't be a passive victim of circumstance and let life drag you around. You will miss the good stuff and it will show in your attitude and your mindset. If everyone else around you is having fun and you are not, you won't feel great. Get in the game of life, *your life*. Refer back to Chapter 3 about spending time with positive people who believe in you and want to see you succeed. They will help you and push you just a little (or a lot, depending on what kind of push you need). Just begin your journey to fun *today*.

●●
"Do more of what makes you awesome."
●●

5

Set the goals, start planning, and create a new path.

Do I Set Short-Term and Long-Term Goals for Myself?

Goals give us forward momentum in our lives, moving us out of our comfort zone and challenging us to be better in all areas. In this chapter, we'll focus on goal-setting, because setting any type of goal, no matter how small, will help you get to a better place. I encourage you to write down your goals and decide on the smaller steps you will take to keep focused and moving in the right direction. I'll explain how to hold yourself accountable for follow-through, and I emphasize that you need to put in the requisite amount of time on research before you embark on a new journey. Sometimes the best outcomes arise from achieving a different goal than the one you set, or achieving the desired goal in an unexpected way. Let's get started.

Are you in the habit of setting short-term and long-term goals for yourself? Or should I just ask you, "Do you have anything to look forward to?"

If, after reading this far, you now believe that you *can* create the life you have always wanted, setting goals is a good way to almost guarantee you will head in the right direction. Envision your journey toward your goal. Map it out. Plan it. Goal-setting works like a map to your good life. If you achieve one goal, then you will be one step closer to living your ideal life!

Don't get stressed by the idea of goal-setting

Setting any type of goal that's going to get you to a better place is a good goal, no matter how small it may be.

- If I achieve my master's degree, then a good job with benefits awaits.
- If I lose the thirty-five pounds, then I will feel better emotionally and physically.

- If I rekindle my love for drawing, then I get the positive benefits of doing what I love (and lower my stress level, too!).

When was the last time you set a goal? Did you achieve it? Goals give us forward momentum in our lives; they challenge us to be better in all areas. Goals move us out of our comfort zone in the pursuit of more and better.

However, so many of us neglect this area of our lives. There's a train of thought that says: "Why set goals if I can never achieve them?" My response is this: Were you in touch with reality when you set those goals, or do you wish for something unrealistic? I love the saying "anything is possible," and although I believe that to be true, it is true within reason. If you want to be president someday and you are a sixty-five-year-old art teacher with no political experience, you may not achieve that goal despite your belief that "anything is possible." However, when your goals are within reason and reach, it is possible. You just need motivation, a strong positive support circle, and the drive to make it happen.

A mistake that many people make is putting all their energy into one goal with no deviation line. If a particular goal doesn't work out, it's all or nothing, and giving up is next. Remember, though, that sometimes the best results come from Plan B. Just because you didn't get accepted into the college of your dreams doesn't mean you won't have an even better experience at another college. In your life, think about how many unanswered prayers you sent up and then gave a silent *Thank You* when the second- or third-choice option actually turned out to be the better one. Plan B or Plan C can be just as good. Think of all the relationships you have had in your past; heartbroken as you were when those ended, looking back, aren't you happy about it now? When you set realistic goals that you want to achieve — new job, new career, hobbies, weight loss, moving to a new city, finding love, etc. — you have to take the small steps that help you work up to the final goal. When you don't do that, you tend to have less success. Here's an example of what I mean.

Joan and Jill want to lose weight, both are excited and motivated. Joan sets up her eating schedule, plans her food every day, and keeps track of her eating. She joins a gym and plans her workouts for three times a week. She gets a babysitter for her daughter so she can meet with a trainer once a week. Joan begins to lose weight and feel great. She regains her self-confidence and enjoys the compliments she receives.

Jill is excited but focuses on "being good" in regards to her food choices, and eats at her work cafeteria every day hoping there will be something "healthy" on the menu. She gets to the gym after work when she can remember to pack her gym bag. She knows she should just pack the bag the night before, but she doesn't. She is initially very confident she can follow through with her goal, despite not breaking it into tiny steps with concrete actions. She soon feels like she can never do anything right, and her self-confidence takes a hit. She gives up.

When you set your mind to a particular goal, you have to do the planning, the documenting, and the brainstorming. You can't just wing it and hope to succeed. There are so many things that can get in the way to get you off track, mainly that thing called Life. Life can throw you off track; don't be naive enough to think it won't happen. That's where the tiny steps can make all the difference between sticking with something and giving up. If you want a better, more fulfilling life, set the goals to get you moving in that direction.

There's a huge difference between wishing for a better life and actually creating it.

When life is tough and not going your way, I wish for you the courage to change it! If you are tired of going to a job you hate, or never having enough money to take a nice vacation, change it! Set the goals, start planning, and create a new path. If you have something you have always wanted to do, don't give it up! Maybe there is a way to make it work! What I hate to hear is "My goal was always to do x, and now it's too late." For that reason, why would you live with regret? It's not too late if you start now. Many of us actually do set mini goals for ourselves all the time, but they are not written down and they are not momentous. These little goals look like this (notice how some of them are not very specific):

- "Let's see how many steps I can do today with my Fitbit."
- "I want to drink my eight glasses of water today."
- "I want to cut my cigarette intake in half this week."
- "I'm making my coffee today not buying it, trying to save money this week."

Success! It happens and we move on, sometimes upping the ante a bit, and other times just feeling good we made it happen. So try doing this on a larger scale.

What else can you accomplish when you put your mind to it? It may take additional resources to help you achieve these larger goals, but the feeling of loving your life, every aspect of it, is a feeling you won't want to miss out on.

Please put in the requisite amount of time on research before embarking on a new journey. Everyone out there is trying to sell you a "quick way to get rich" program or a "new certificate program that will get you a financially stable career." Not every "looks almost too good" program is worth your time. If you are going to put your time and money into something, be sure it will have the rewards you are looking for. Don't get caught in the trap of allowing people to lure you in without researching companies, career paths, and so forth. What would be your return on investment? Will you go into debt? How much in loans can you realistically manage? Be careful and realistic. Don't further complicate your life. Talk to the people in your life, especially the positive but realistic ones. Map it all out. If it feels right, then take the chance. Remember, your time and money are precious, so make sure it will be worth it. Don't choose the easy way out with hopes you will get the same rewards as someone else who will work very hard.

Ask yourself these questions:

- If I achieve my goals, how will my life change for the better?
- If I imagine my goals are achieved and I am in a much better place in my life, how do I feel?
- What if I never try?
- How will I feel then?

Don't have the "*that could have been me*" phrase ready to fire out at someone who is working hard at making their dreams come true.

This is your life we are talking about.

Be open to the idea that it could and will happen for you! As my fortune cookie once read, "Don't be pushed by your problems, be led by your dreams."

When you think about goal-setting, think about all the areas in your life where you may feel a little stuck, or maybe about the long term, such as where you want to be in five years. If you wait for five years to go by before you act, you will be right where you are today, just five years older. Start the process now. Here are some examples of broad, general goals in the key areas of your life. Note that the more you can create "SMART" goals — goals that are specific, measurable/meaningful, attainable, realistic, and time-based (have a deadline) — the greater your likelihood of success.

- *Spiritual:* Read more books; return to faith; practice yoga or mediation; go on retreats (to India or in your backyard, it doesn't matter).
- *Physical:* Start a new exercise routine or return to a previous one; concentrate on better eating and healthy cooking; explore new workouts; go to the doctor for an annual physical; focus on weight loss or getting stronger.
- *Emotional:* Find a therapist to help you deal with past issues; meet new friends or a new love; try new hobbies or return to old favorites.
- *Professional:* Look for new employment; switch to a new career; go back to school; read; take certificate courses; find a mentor and/or be a mentor.

Think about your goal and the smaller steps needed to keep you focused and moving in the right direction. Let's set some goals!

Short-Term Goals

1-week goals

A. ....

B. ....

C. ....

1-month goals

A. ....

B. ....

C. ....

3-month goals

A. ....

B. ....

C. ....

Long-Term Goals

What are my one- to five-year goals? For example, if you would like to buy a nice sports car, something you have always wanted but have never had the money to purchase, what about in five years? Most likely if you are doing nothing to accomplish this goal in your day-to-day life, in five years you still will be wishing for it. If you plan now the simple steps to guide yourself, you just might get your dream-come-true vehicle (or vacation home, or being debt-free, etc.). Here's how to break it down.

GOAL: Buy a sports car

When: Five years from now

Small steps

1. Research how much it will cost you.
2. Is this a realistic goal for you to obtain?
3. Review your finances and decide
   A. Do I need to get another job?
   B. Do I need to take money each week and put it in a special car savings account?
   C. Where should I cut back on my spending?

Each year you should review your progress. You might get that car sooner than five years or adjust your goal to six or seven years. Either way you look at it, you have a plan and are working towards your goal. How good will it feel to be riding around in your dream car? I bet it will feel amazing.

You get the picture on how setting up the goals and smaller steps can really work to keep you on track. Try it.

Ask yourself these questions:

- What do I have to look forward to this week?
- When was the last time I got really excited about something I planned and achieved?
- Do I remember how it felt to achieve my goal? What were the feelings associated with achievement?
- Am I ready now to set new goals?
- What do I need to put in my life so I can focus and get excited about a new adventure?
- Who do I need help or support from to help with my success?

Think of someone you admire. Famous or not, what are the qualities about them you admire? Did you ever think about how they got to be where they are today? What do you think his/her goals were? I love to hear, "wow, look at how far they have come despite all the setbacks they had!" You know what that means? They had obstacles, things got in their way many times as they tried to pursue their goals, but they persevered. They didn't quit, because they wanted it so badly.

It is possible based on how badly you want it to happen. If it means a lot to you, pursue it.

Get ready for the challenges and obstacles, because life is full of them. Take, for example, my friend Jean, a single mother who knew she needed to go back to school to advance and get a good-paying job. To her, the thought of actually going to school was overwhelming. She spent some time speaking with peers in the jobs she wanted, gathering information about what the requirements would be and how to begin the process. The meeting with a college counselor was what gave her the big boost she needed and shifted her dreams into doable goals. She was eligible for loans and most of her required classes were available online. Halfway through her second semester, life threw her a curveball so she had to put her dreams on hold temporarily. She was devastated. (This is where many of us lose momentum and stop.) However, the minute Jean could start up again she did, with even more determination to make it work. She could easily predict her future if she stayed where she was, and it wasn't at all easy or rewarding.

After four years of studying into the late-night hours, caring for her children, and working a minimum-wage job, Jean finally entered the workforce as a professional. Her job now provides her with reimbursement for more college classes and paid vacation time! Each time I see her, I remind her how amazing she is for chasing that dream of hers until it became real. Those old words, as cliché as they might sound, "go for it, don't quit on your dreams, you can do it," are truly packed with meaning and truth.

Here's another example. For the past fifteen years, Doug has worked in a job he used to love. He stays because it's all he knows, even though he stopped enjoying his work about five years ago. He knows every person at the small company and he doesn't like any of them. It's a chore to go to work each day with a bad attitude. He has had many job offers in the past because he is very skilled at what he does, but Doug is comfortable with his current job. He complains to anyone who will listen, and when encouraged to find a new job that he loves, he makes excuses and really just can't move past the fear of the unknown. He is not alone. Many of us stay in situations because it's comfortable and it's all we know. Once we love a job, it's natural for us to think it will work out for the long haul and the need to set new goals flies out the window. My advice to you, if you see yourself in any part of Doug's story — fear, unknown, comfort zone, easy, complaining — please do yourself a favor. Take a vacation and set some new career goals. You do yourself and everyone around you no favors by staying in a job you dislike.

When Minor Setbacks Become Major Obstacles

You have finally made an effort to lose weight, go back to school, start looking for a new job, or find a therapist. Then the unexpected happens. You hurt your foot. Your spouse needs surgery. Your babysitter quits. Your student loan falls through. Although such events might have an impact on you and cause you to pause for a moment, maybe even throw you off course for a little while, they should not completely derail you.

This is where your resilient self comes into play. You know, that's the part of you that feels temporarily let down, but then picks up the pieces with more dedication to completing what was initially started. You can find new ways to figure it out. Ask people for their support, ideas, and help with problem-solving. Resilient people pick up the pieces and keep moving forward. They focus on finding another way, open to the idea that maybe Plan C and Plan D might work.

Folks who are not too resilient tend to crumble and go off course indefinitely, often leaving behind broken dreams and half-achieved goals along the way.

Put your effort into developing your resilient coping skills. How much time do you devote to your well-being? I don't mean watching the television when the kids are out playing day after day. I'm talking about truly developing yourself in a positive way. Are you a better person now than you were last year? What have you done? Have you accomplished any personal goals, dedicated time to personal growth, taken new classes, read any inspiring books? If not, what are you doing? Too much time on Facebook? Watching bad TV? Hanging out with people who are immature, self-absorbed, and ignorant?

Put time into getting yourself emotionally stronger. Resilience is a skill set that must be worked on all the time. How can you afford not to? Life is full of unexpected twists and turns and you have to be ready to change direction but not lose sight of your commitments and your goals.

Invest in yourself. Spending all day at the gym is just one small piece of self-care; remember that you need to also focus on your mind. What's happening on the inside? What issues might need to be resolved from childhood, the ones that continue to rear their heads in the form of depression, fear, and self-loathing? Do the work. Invite joy in. Ask yourself these questions:

- What's my purpose?
- What do I love to do?
- What feeds my soul?
- When was the last time I tried something new?

Use that much-needed quiet refection time to focus on your self-care skills. Inner strength can set you free of the little annoying stuff that tempts you to stay still, to quit, to forget about your personal goals, to go backwards. Work on it. Put yourself first. Your happiness is worth it.

Diane Fraser, author of *Growing Up Superheroes: The Extraordinary Adventures of Deihlia Nye*, helps others experience life on a spiritual level, and reconnect to their own motivation, dreams, and personal magic. She writes,

> *"When you really enjoy who you are, the universe picks up on it and gives you more ways to experience yourself, to grow, to express yourself. You'll attract people and situations to you that are a really good fit, rather than attracting things that require you to change and contort yourself in order to make it work. When you're in a good place with yourself, it will be reflected in everything around you. And when drama hits or things come up, you can handle them more easily because you are centered correctly — in yourself."*

There is a strong link between self-esteem and goal-setting. In this chapter, we've focused on setting goals, stepping outside your comfort zone, and welcoming new experiences in. The other piece of this, often the missing piece as to why these goals never seem to take flight, is the inner work that you must do. If you don't do this work, the achieving and striving turns into not starting and never accomplishing. As my friend Deb so eloquently put it:

Last July I woke up one morning and decided to change my life for the better. I was very depressed; although I always had a smile on my face, I was crying on the inside. I never got over losing my mom, but I have learned that I have to accept it and know she is always with me. I was very unhappy with myself and "just let myself go." I realized that if I wanted to be a better mom for my kids I had to be a better person to myself first. I knew if I wanted to change then I would have to do it myself, no one was going to do it for me. I have worked very hard over the last year to get to where I am today. You're never too old and it's never too late to make a change!

Love yourself enough to want the best for you, stop looking at others achieving their dreams and feeling bad for yourself. This is your time, let this book inspire you to take action. The right time is right now!

•••••••••••••••••••••••••••••••••••••••
"When you know what you want, and you want it bad enough, you'll find a way to get it." —Jim Rohn
•••••••••••••••••••••••••••••••••••••••

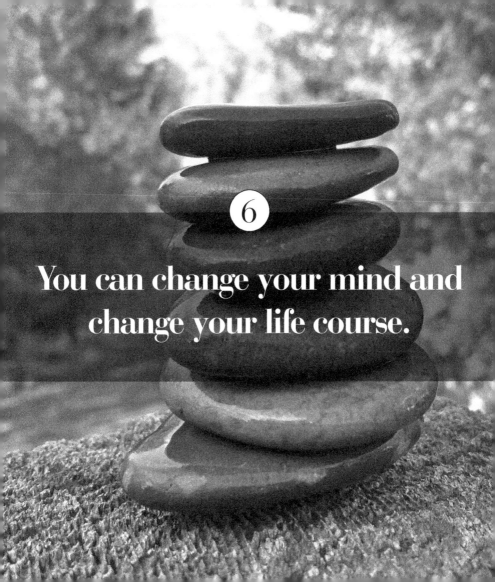

6

You can change your mind and change your life course.

Am I Creating the Life that I Want?

t's time to envision and create the life you want, instead of blaming and making excuses. Think about your choices and how you might learn from past mistakes. Don't keep repeating the same pattern if it is not working. It is never too late to change your ways to adopt a healthier lifestyle, for example, or to stop making choices that directly conflict with how you want your life to be. Don't wish and want only to be frustrated when the change doesn't happen. Don't give up on finding what you want if you have not yet even started the process of finding it. Creating the life you want takes work and courage. Let's start putting all the pieces together.

Create: (verb)
to bring something into existence.

Ask yourself, am I creating the life that I want?

OR am I (check all that apply):
- [ ] Making excuses
- [ ] Blaming others for not getting what I want
- [ ] Being a passive victim of circumstance (life hates me!)
- [ ] Prefer complaining to actually doing

Ask yourself: Am I creating the life I want? What am I really doing with myself exactly? What do I do every day to get me closer to my ideal life situation?

Have you ever heard the quote that says, "Do something your future self will thank you for"? Think about that for a minute, about doing something now that later in life you will be so thankful you did! That could be going to college, starting to work at a company that you know in years to come will be so beneficial, investing in the stock market, and (one of my biggest, most important things that I believe everyone can do right now) getting healthy.

Although this is not a "get healthy" book, it sort of is, and here's why. If you put all the pieces together in your life so that you can enjoy life later, but you are not taking care of your health today (smoking, overweight, addiction, no exercise) ask yourself how much can you really enjoy without good health? The rewards of focusing on health will far outweigh the struggle now, I guarantee it! It can be a dramatic and at times seemingly impossible struggle to get your health under control, but waiting and not doing anything about it will only make the situation worse in the future.

It's natural to look at others with envious eyes, wishing that somehow you could have a piece of their life, maybe their home, vacations, good marriage, their job, their schedule, their babysitters, their patience, their ability to get to the gym every day, their nice yard, their friends, their pool...and the list goes on and on. That's okay, as long as you decide *how* you *will* put that in your life. Looking and envying won't get you that great schedule, the job or the friends. It's all the work that goes into making your life wonderful for *you* that can be a roadblock for so many of us.

Does this sound familiar? Year after year passes when you are just wishing instead of creating, and you are still stuck in the same place, without what you envision as a better life. Or maybe you're focusing on the wrong stuff, the life stuff that keeps you in the same place or moves you backwards from the life you want to create. Sometimes it is just so much of a routine we don't even realize we are moving backwards. Other times we may have an idea that what we are doing in our daily life is just all we know right now. Be easy with yourself, be patient. Change is hard, and most often difficult.

In the previous chapters, I've offered you some ideas to get you moving and creating your wonderful life, but you also need courage and diligence. Some people in your life may not be thrilled when you leave them behind as you propel yourself forward. In fact, as they see you getting excited and even glowing as you connect with your authentic self and align yourself with what you have always wanted (and believe you deserve!), they may try to pull you down. Don't let them. They can also have what you have. Get excited when you look at others whom you want to emulate and think with eager eyes and open heart,

* *
"How can I also tap into that?"
* *

Don't do this with jealousy or envy, don't start the sentence with "I wish I could be like …" or "I wish I could have…" Instead, start the sentence with "I would like to create my life in such a way that I go on vacation once a year," or "I would like to create my life in such a way that I have a shorter commute so I have more family time."

If you allow someone else to create your life, you won't get what *you* want, you will get what *they want for you*. Will these match up? Not necessarily. You may join them in setting up your life and enjoy the ride for a while, then realize at some point, "this wasn't the life I envisioned myself having." Remember, people will always tell you what you "should be doing." They can even find ways for you to fill up your time, but you ultimately control your life. You have the power to reject those ideas and options and go with one of your own. It's your life to create. You must have some idea by now of what you want. What would bring you joy, and what or who does not? Start there. If you do not know which direction you need to go, spend some time thinking about it. Turn the computer off — Facebook won't tell you how you will get a better life, it might just make you frustrated looking at everyone else's! Turn your phone off, and spend some time alone thinking about these questions:

- What would your ideal life look like?
- What would you put in it?
- Who would you leave out?
- How would you structure your day?
- What might you need more time for?

When you think about the answers to the above questions, you might start feeling excited, like a spark within you has been ignited. You might think, "Yes! What if I could plan each day exactly how I want it to be?" Imagine that! Taking control of your circumstances and allowing yourself to think about your ideal life is super-exciting! Start writing down all that comes to mind. Make list after list, and when you come up with new ideas, write them down too. Keep brainstorming about all the things you want to place in your life to make it better and more satisfying.

When we are young we have *big dreams* of the job, house, vacations, career, and family we want. Then as we age, if we happen to get locked into or stuck in a particular situation, we feel as though life has taken a firm grip on us and doesn't want to let up. Deflated and disappointed, many of us just trudge through the mud of our daily lives without ever bringing back the goals and dreams of youth. I believe the wonderful benefit of getting older is you become wiser about your own needs and wants, the very specifics of what you like and dislike.

In youth, we dream big but can sometimes lack the insight to actually achieve it all. Now, older, we carry the insight but lack the skills to achieve the life we really truly want. Don't be afraid to change direction in your life. What are you waiting for? You are not too old, too young, too stuck, because everyone can rediscover themselves at any age at any point in their life. You can change your mind and therefore change your life course. Will it be challenging? Could be. Will it be worth it? *Yes!* Using all the information in this book will give you a good start and help propel you forward. Rally your supportive friends, tell them your ideas, get excited and use that momentum to keep you going even when setbacks occur. It's exciting to think you can create the life you have always imagined! Get working on setting short-term and long-term goals that will help you to create the life you want. Think ahead, and say to yourself:

Here's where I want to be in five to ten years and this is what I have to do now to make it happen. (Write it down!)

In the meantime, having smaller, short-term goals will keep you focused and feeling enthusiastic about your life. There is so much to learn and see, and there are so many ways to grow. Your job is to allow room in your life for all of it!

- Keep an open mind, life may surprise you!
- You might need to break your routine and try something new.
- Let go of feeling selfish about wanting a great life, go get it and be proud!
- Let go of friends who are negative.
- Dream big, and don't stop until you have achieved what you envisioned.
- Check and readjust your goals and dreams as you gain more insight into what you want.
- Believe you are worthy of having what you want.
- Every day, are you doing at least one thing that brings you closer to your ideal life? (This might be saving money, saying "no," job hunting, or trying new hobbies.)
- Ask yourself, is this where I want to be in my life?
- At this point in my life, are there changes I need to make in order to feel more fulfilled?
- What small step in pursuing my dreams might be the best for me today?

- After reviewing all the chapters and my answers to the questions in this book, what do I need to focus on to get me to a better place?
- What do I have to work on that might be a potential setback for me?

Creating your life exactly as you want it to be takes bringing positive people into your social circle, setting short-term and long-term goals, being mindful of where and how you spend your time, and doing things you love. I find that people often give up too easily. I see lots of enthusiasm at first, when the thought permeates their mind that "*Yes*, I actually *can* have the life I want!" It's all very exciting and motivating until you bump up against the first hurdle, and you lose momentum and gain nothing but disappointment and confirmation that the world is against you living a good life. You may be laughing at this exaggerated line of thinking, but it is very true for many people. Handling adversity isn't their strong suit, so giving up is easier and takes less time.

No More Excuses, Start Reflecting and Moving Forward

Each year I host my beautiful and inspiring Women's Weekend where women gather from all over to come together for joy, friendship, and personal growth. At this event, the sponsors and speakers share their brilliant expertise and offer incredible gifts that the women can access. Throughout the weekend, I often over-hear "I really have to call her," "I really NEED to call her," "I would love to work with her on my _____ issue" or try out that treatment, exercise, etc.

I hear it all the time — the wanting, the longing to try something new, the excitement about possibilities.

And then unfortunately, after the weekend concludes, the impetus to take action begins to fizzle out. That "I'm going to" begins to sound something like "I really should take that class," "I really liked her, maybe I will call her and try out that treatment, exercise, service, etc."

Then a week or two goes by and the inner dialogue changes to "I just don't have the time," "It wouldn't work anyway," "I don't have the money" and "I don't leave my comfort zone, it's safe here."

Ah, the excuses! I have heard them all. And they really frustrate me because the excuses keep us from living and following up on the excitement and action that can improve our lives. So I'm going to tell you what you need to do about it.

Right now — try stopping for a moment and reflecting. This can be very hard to do if you are connected to social media 24/7; there's always gossip to share and other people's lives to view and envy. But truly stop and reflect on those people, activities or experiences you really want to be involved with, but have made excuses about not following through.

Ask yourself, will it (the person, activity, experience) make me a better person? Will it help me move past my pain and create a better future for me? Will saving money for this allow me to achieve a goal in my life? Do I need to set new goals?

Try reflection — a lost practice, an often neglected place to be. Sitting idle with your own thoughts can be scary for those of us who might actually uncover some hidden past hurt to be resolved or dreams we've been afraid to start pursuing for fear of failure. Let me help you. Sitting quietly, start your morning or end your day or anytime in between, just simply ask yourself these important questions:

- How am I doing?
- Am I satisfied with my life?
- Am I content in my life?
- Would I like to try something new?

Try it if you can find peace in your own thoughts. You have the key to make those changes. It first has to come from within you — a longing for something different, a dream that has been burning slowly under your skin, a goal you have had since you were a child, just waiting to be accomplished. Life is busy, pushing aside even the best of intentions.

With much reflection on what has been missing in her life, my sweet friend Jane decided it was her faith and spirituality that was missing in her life. She was raised Catholic, but was called to a different church and a different religion. She found connection, spirituality, and friendship in a small Christian church. She decided this was a missing link in her life and began the journey to become baptized. Her life feels fuller and she feels confident that it is where she has been meant to be. Her decision took courage to follow her heart and an adventurous spirit to allow her faith to show her the way.

What's your missing link? What would bring you more fulfillment in your life? Where will your journey take you? How will you know if you don't ask yourself over and over again — answers are revealed in time, not necessarily immediately. Don't get frustrated. Just sit with it. Be patient. The answers will always come. Once they come to you, be prepared to move in a new direction, and set those excuses aside.

Reflect on it.

The biggest mistake people make is sitting back, wishing and wanting, and then getting frustrated when the desired change doesn't happen. That's when people turn sour, dismayed and disillusioned with their life. I often hear people say, "Well it just wasn't meant to be for me" when they haven't even tried to make it happen. Certain things may not be meant to be, but how will you know if you don't work for it? Don't give up on finding the right job, the amazing lover, the dream house, the perfect vacation, time for yourself, family time, friend time, if you have never even started the process. It takes work to create. It takes courage to create. It also means taking the good with the bad, the easy with the challenges, and not feeling defeated when one door closes. People don't get handed "an amazing life," they have to work for it. They work at putting all the pieces together in a way that feels right to them.

Is it selfish for you to create the life you want? No! No way! If you are living an amazing life, it benefits everyone around you. Think of those bad, cranky days where nothing goes right, when you are irritable and annoyed at everyone and everything. Who wants to be near you then? Not even you! I'm not saying you will never have a bad day when you live and do what you love, but I can tell you that you will shine brighter. You will feel consistently content, successful and empowered. Everyone around you will feel that too. Your positive impact will be felt by everyone.

shine on

Here's a big question you may be asking yourself right now: How do I take the focus off of others and put it on me without feeling guilty, when that is what I have always done and have created as part of my life? Everyone else first, me last. It might be hard, but not impossible to break this mindset. Be realistic about what will change in your life and how it will impact those around you. If you can't make big changes right now (new career, new home, vacation home, retirement), how about making small changes to help you slowly get to where you need to be? That is still progress in the right direction. For example, you don't want to put yourself or family into debt to go back to college, but maybe taking just one or two classes per semester can get you moving in the direction of that college degree you always wanted. Sometimes we have to adjust our timelines and expectations, so be flexible. Be patient. Moving slowly but surely will get you there — but you have to start *now* or you will go nowhere very fast.

Ask yourself, and answer honestly: Am I creating the life I want, or complicating it? I often see people making life harder for themselves by making choices that don't fit correctly or that complicate it (whether it be accepting long commutes in favor of money, feeling that having a miserable lover is better than being alone, or volunteering all their free time for something that only brings them frustration). The big and small choices we make, if they are not directly in line with our lifestyle and how we want to create a really good life, can halt the process of change and actually reverse it, making us angry, frustrated, and stressed.

Think about your choices, and learn from past mistakes. Don't keep repeating the same pattern if it is not working for you. It is never too late to change your ways to adopt a healthier lifestyle. Get to a point in your life where you are willing to fight hard for your life. Are you making choices that are in direct conflict with how you want your life to be? Is it a pattern for you to continue making such choices even though you know they might not be the best choices for you?

As I said earlier in Chapter 1, some people struggle with mental illness (including depression and severe anxiety), and other serious issues. Don't take any of these conditions lightly, especially if you just can't seem to make the right decisions. This may be based in how you grew up and on other unresolved issues you may have experienced or are experiencing currently. Please, speak with your primary care physician or your insurance company to get referrals to a good therapist in your area who can help you work this out. Mental health has to be the top priority if you want everything else to fall into place in your life. When you are in a good emotional space, fill it with what brings you joy, from the people in it right down to the clothing you wear.

The time may never be right, so use this as your daily mantra:

The right time is right now.

Try it: Below, I ask you five times to answer differently. As you answer the question each time, think about the process of creating your life. Are you creating it in such a way that allows you more time for you? More friendships? The ability to only bring positive people in your life? Having a rewarding career? Less depression? More happiness? These answers bring out the totality of your life.

1. I would like to create my life in such a way that I

2. I would like to create my life in such a way that I

3. I would like to create my life in such a way that I

4. I would like to create my life in such a way that I

5. I would like to create my life in such a way that I

Starting right now, I can do the following, which will allow me to create the life I love and have always imagined:

1.

2.

3.

4.

5.

Am I creating the life that I want? All the chapters in this book are so vitally important in helping you to figure out what might be the one piece you are missing.

This chapter has focused on key questions:

- Am I moving in the right direction?
- Which direction am I heading in my life?
- What will bring me a life of fulfillment?

I know this chapter has many one-sentence, simple, positive sayings like "Let go of feeling selfish because you want a great life, go get it and be proud!" and "Dream big, don't stop until you have achieved what you envisioned." They may seem so simple and clichéd; however, if you take even one of them to heart, think about it, meditate on it, use it as your daily mantra, one short sentence can have a positive impact on your thought process throughout the day. One of my favorite ideas in this chapter is this: *The biggest mistake people make is sitting back, wishing and wanting, and then getting frustrated when the change doesn't happen.* That's really my main reason for writing this book and sharing it with you: Don't wait, because

The Right Time Is Right Now.

> *"Your life does not get better by chance, it gets better by change." –Jim Rohn*

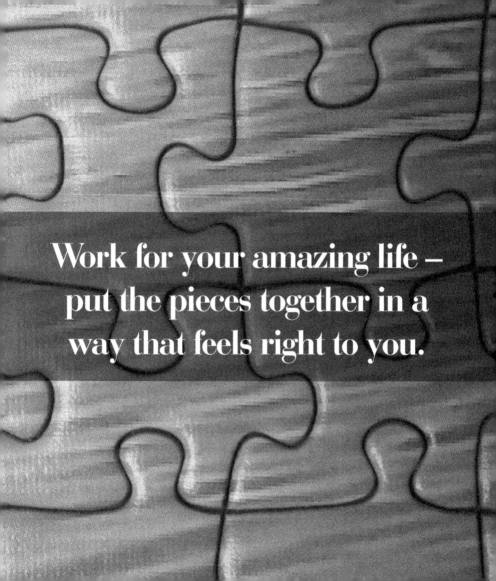

Work for your amazing life –
put the pieces together in a
way that feels right to you.

Conclusion

Life has a way of throwing us off balance every chance it gets. When we think we just about have it all together, a curve ball flies in so fast and furious the whole world can turn upside down. I hope this book has reminded you that you can still make those goals and dreams come true, even if life has beat them up a little here and there. I urge you to start creating the life you want, beginning with a check on self-esteem and self-confidence. I encourage you, my reader, to find help dealing with any mental health issues that may be preventing you from moving forward in life. When we feel balanced emotionally, we are ready to take on the world.

The six questions in this book are meant as a personal guide for you if you don't feel content and might not be able to determine why. I encourage you to be patient, as it takes courage and determination to implement changes. As we begin to set new goals (or even bring back old goals stuffed in the closet with dust and regret), sometimes the challenge is keeping the momentum going.

Let's take a quick look at what we covered in this book.

Chapter 1 — Question 1:
Am I Engaged in Work That I Love?

This first question sets the tone for the book. I ask you to think about whether the work you do every day — whatever it may be — is something you love, and whether the answer is love, hate, or indifference, how that affects your life. When we are doing something that we love, we feel good. We are happier and more invested in our lives. If we hate our everyday routine, we cannot help but feel drained and frustrated. Ask yourself whether you are living for the weekends and dreading the weekdays or the opposite, and know that it doesn't have to be that way. What if we felt great about what we do *every* day? If the thought of making small or big changes in your life feels overwhelming, be reassured that each chapter walks you through a step in the process of creating a life you love. With the belief that there's plenty of joy to go around, this book guides you to the steps you can take so you love what you do.

Chapter 2 — Question 2:
Where Do I Spend My Time?

When the discussion turns to living a fulfilling life, too often the phrase "not enough time" is the response. Everyone has enough time to play, rest, reflect, refresh, laugh and daydream. If you laugh at that statement, you just may *really* need to answer this question: Where and how do you spend your time? Even busy people can still make the time to play and have time to themselves. It's all in who or what is taking our time and how well we manage the time that we have. Instead of delivering a lecture on time management, I take you through a series of questions and prompts that encourage you to stop *wishing* you had more time for the fun things you would like to do and to start *making* the time.

Chapter 3 — Question 3:
Do I Have Supportive People in My Social Circle?

We all need support and true friendship in our lives, as friendship is nourishment for the soul. In fact, not having the support of those around us is often the biggest obstacle to achieving our goals and dreams. Negative comments from negative people can keep us at a standstill. Fearful people can infect us with that same disease and we become paralyzed, afraid of new ideas. However, having friends, confidants, mentors or business partners with a positive, bright attitude can not only get us moving but also keep us moving when we need it most. This chapter prompts you to examine how supportive your social circle is, and encourages you to ask for help and support.

Chapter 4 — Question 4:
Do I Regularly Participate in Activities that Bring Me Joy?

In this chapter, I ask you to reflect on whether you have favorite activities you regularly participate in once a week, if not more often. No one is exempt from enjoying themselves. What fun is life when it becomes all work and no play? If it's all chores and the daily grind, fulfillment may be hard to find. I remind you how important it is to have fun, especially when other parts of your life aren't going so well. Hobbies and other enjoyable activities are important because they can take us away for just a little bit, making us feel a little less stressed and a lot more fulfilled. They remind us that there is fun to be had or a sense of accomplishment to be found, even when we feel like all is not headed in a good direction. When we engage in what we love, it's like an electric charge of joy goes right to the soul. Fully participating in life means taking chances, meeting new people, and trying new activities. I urge you to open yourself up to adventure.

Chapter 5 — Question 5:
Do I Set Short-Term and Long-Term Goals for Myself?

Goals give us forward momentum in our lives, moving us out of our comfort zone and challenging us to be better in all areas. In this chapter focused on goal-setting, I remind you that setting any type of goal that will help you get to a better place is a good goal, no matter how small it may be. Write down your goals and decide on the smaller steps you will take to keep focused and moving in the right direction. You'll learn how to hold yourself accountable for follow-through, and be reminded to put in the requisite amount of time on research before embarking on a new journey. One of the most common mistakes people make is to focus all their energy on one goal with no deviation line. For some, if a particular goal doesn't work out, the all-or-nothing mindset means giving up is next, but sometimes the best outcomes arise from achieving a different goal or achieving the desired goal in an unexpected way.

Chapter 6 — Question 6:
Am I Creating the Life that I Want?

This chapter encourages you to envision and create the life you want, instead of blaming and making excuses. Prompted by open-ended questions and statements to complete, you get to think about your choices and how you might learn from past mistakes. Don't keep repeating the same pattern if it is not working. It is never too late to change our ways to adopt a healthier lifestyle, for example, or to stop making choices that directly conflict with how we want our life to be. The biggest mistake people make is sitting back, wishing and wanting, then getting frustrated when the change doesn't happen. That's when people turn sour, dismayed, and disillusioned with their lives. I encourage you not to give up on finding what you want if you have not yet even started the process. It takes work and courage to create the life we want. It also means taking the good with the bad, the easy with the challenges, and not feeling defeated when one door closes. We don't get handed "an amazing life" — we have to work for it, putting all the pieces together in a way that feels right to us.

With Joy and best wishes as you embark on this journey,

Julie McGrath

Julie McGrath

About the Author

Julie McGrath is a Licensed Independent Clinical Social Worker who has worked in the mental health field for the past 17 years. She is currently the director of a crisis team in a hospital emergency department north of Boston, connected to the world-renowned Massachusetts General Hospital and Brigham and Women's Hospital in Boston, Massachusetts. She manages a busy department of crisis clinicians, arranges for the care and placement of the mental health and/or substance-abusing patient, and advocates for patients' needs within the larger systems throughout the state.

Julie created The Joy Source in 2009, focused on empowering women to find their joy, purpose and passion, and go live it! She published her first book, *Joy-Worthy, A Mother's Guide to More Joy, Less Stress and No Guilt*, in 2012. She hosts a Women's Getaway Weekend every spring to inspire and rejuvenate women from all over the country.

Through her activities as a social worker, she has created Julie McGrath Seminars, a public speaking business that serves human services professionals, nurses, physicians, social workers, and counselors. She speaks regularly to groups of up to 300 people on such topics such as job stress, burnout, self-care, working with difficult people, time management, and setting boundaries. In these workshops, Julie brilliantly combines work and home life to inspire her participants to seek the good life professionally and personally. That "good life" involves setting and achieving goals, and practicing effective time management so life includes work and play time, as well as appropriate amounts of rest and relaxation. Because she captivates audiences with her dynamic style and humor, she is in high demand for professional development days, keynotes and full-day seminars.

For more information and inspiration, visit www.thejoysource.com or follow The Joy Source on Facebook.

Contact Julie at julie@thejoysource.com or 978-854-6935.

For more information

For further information on upcoming events, reach out to me at:
Julie@thejoysource.com

Or, visit my websites:
www.juliemcgrath.com
www.thejoysource.com

www.facebook.com/TheJoySource

@thejoysource

Julie McGrath, LICSW